RAID AT ENTEBBE

IRA PECK

SCHOLASTIC BOOK SERVICES
New York Toronto London Auckland Sydney Tokyo

No part of this publication may be reproduced in whole or in part, or stored in a retrieval system, or transmitted in any form or by any means, electronic, mechanical, photocopying, recording, or otherwise, without written permission of the publisher. For information regarding permission, write to Scholastic Book Services, 50 West 44th Street, New York, NY 10036.

Copyright © 1977 by Scholastic Magazines, Inc. All rights reserved. Published by Scholastic Book Services, a division of Scholastic Magazines, Inc.

12 11 10 9 8 7 6 5 4 3 2 1   4   7 8 9/7 0 1 2/8
              Printed in the U.S.A.   06

CONTENTS

Bantam Books

Simulated attack: Israeli airborne commandos race from transport plane during maneuvers.

I

THE STAKES
AT ENTEBBE

On July 4, 1976, while Americans were celebrating their nation's Bicentennial, the people of Israel were rejoicing in an event that they also saw as a triumph for freedom and independence. Only the night before, Israeli airborne commandos had carried out one of the most audacious and spectacular missions ever conceived, freeing 103 hostages held by terrorists at Entebbe, Uganda. The hostages were Israeli citizens who had been aboard an Air France jetliner when it was hijacked en route to Paris from Tel Aviv. The terrorists were agents of the Popular Front for the Liberation of Palestine (PFLP), an Arab nationalist group dedicated to the destruction of Israel. The PFLP had threatened to execute the hostages unless Israel released 40 Arab or pro-Arab terrorists held in its jails. The PFLP also demanded the release of 13 terrorists held by other countries.

When these demands were made, Israel had no way of dealing with the situation militarily. Entebbe is about 2,500 miles from Israel's southernmost air fields. To carry out a military operation at such a distance would require careful planning, and there was little time for that. In fact, the terrorists had given the Israeli government only about 48 hours to meet their demands.

What was the government to do? From past experience, it knew that surrender would only encourage further acts of terrorism. Israelis would be unable to travel anywhere in safety, and the nation would be isolated. To give in now was potentially disastrous. On the other hand, no one wanted 103 Israeli citizens to be slaughtered. Prime Minister Yitzhak Rabin's dilemma was underscored when a crowd of anxious relatives of the hostages besieged his office, demanding or imploring that he yield to the terrorists. Rabin was reminded (as if he didn't know) that the government's refusal to deal with terrorists in the past had sometimes led to tragic consequences.

One such tragedy had shocked the entire world. On September 5, 1972, eight Arab terrorists, members of an extremist group called the Black September, invaded the quarters of Israeli athletes at the Olympic games in Munich, Germany. The Arabs killed two men and held nine others as hostages. They demanded that Israel release 200 terrorist prisoners in exchange for the hostages' lives. Israel, whose government was then headed by Prime Minister Golda Meir, refused to negotiate with them. The responsibility of dealing with the terrorists was left to German authorities.

When persuasion and bribery failed to move the terrorists, the Germans attempted a ruse. They offered to provide the terrorists with a jet airliner that would fly them to any country they named. Presumably the Arabs would be allowed to take their hostages with them. The terrorists and their Israeli hostages were flown to a nearby airport in helicopters. Meanwhile, police sharpshooters had been staked around the airport with orders to pick off the terrorists when they emerged from the helicopters. Strangely, only five men armed with bolt-action rifles were assigned to kill eight terrorists armed with submachine guns and grenades. In the ensuing shootout, the Arabs murdered all their hostages before they themselves were killed or surrendered to the police.

At Ben-Gurion airport near Tel Aviv, a crowd of 3,000 mourners greeted the plane bearing the bodies of the Israeli athletes. Indeed, the whole nation mourned. Now, less than four years later, Israel was confronted with the possibility of an even greater tragedy. The lives of 103 hostages, men, women, and children, were at stake 2,500 miles away in east Africa. What would the government of Israel do? What could it do?

3

II

A NATION
IS BORN

Tragedy, terror, and crises were not new to the people of Israel. In fact, their nation had been born amid these circumstances, and almost seemed to derive its strength from them. As young men, Prime Minister Rabin and other members of the cabinet had fought in Israel's War of Independence (1948-1949) and had vivid memories of the ordeal. They witnessed the heroism, daring, and willingness to sacrifice that carried the Israelis to victory, and they knew that those qualities would not be lacking in other crises.

Oddly, one of the most critical events in the founding of Israel took place a long way from any Mideastern battleground. The scene was the White House in Washington, D.C., where on May

13, 1948, President Harry S. Truman received a letter from Chaim Weizmann, a Jewish statesman. Weizmann was a leader of the Zionist movement to establish a homeland for Jews in Palestine, the site that in ancient times was the home of their Hebrew forebears. The Zionist movement was begun in the 1890's by Jews seeking to escape persecution in Europe. Weizmann reminded President Truman that on the following day British rule in Palestine would come to an end and that a Jewish state, which had been authorized by the United Nations General Assembly, would be created in the area allotted to it. (The General Assembly had voted in 1947 to partition Palestine into two states, one Jewish, the other Arab.) Then Weizmann expressed the wish that was at the heart of his letter:

"I deeply hope that the United States, which under your leadership has done so much to find a just solution [in Palestine], will promptly recognize the Provisional Government of the new Jewish State. The world, I think, will regard it as especially appropriate that the greatest living democracy should be the first to welcome the newest into the family of nations."

Recognition of the new Jewish nation — Israel — had been a knotty problem for the United States. Ironically, the U.S. had been the chief sponsor in the United Nations of an independent Jewish state. But the government had not anticipated the violent reaction that the UN partition plan produced among Arab leaders. To them, the creation of a Jewish state in Palestine was intolerable. *All* of Palestine, they said, belonged under Arab rule.

In Egypt, one Arab leader spoke in strident tones of making war against the proposed Jewish state as soon as British forces pulled out of Palestine. "This will be a war of extermination and a momentous massacre," he declared, "which will be spoken of like the Mongol massacres and the Crusades."

U.S. government leaders began to have second thoughts about the establishment of a Jewish state in Palestine. They were shocked by the depth of Arab hostility to the partition plan. And they doubted whether the Jewish underground army, the Haganah, could defend the state against large-scale Arab invasions. In truth, U.S. leaders feared that there *would* be "a momentous massacre" of the Jewish population, and this was a responsibility that they did not want to have on their hands. By the spring of 1948, the United States had abandoned its support of the UN partition plan and was advocating instead an international trusteeship in Palestine. Under this plan, the Jews in Palestine would have to wait for independence until the Arab nations would accept it — a very remote possibility at best.

Jewish leaders in Palestine were determined not to lose the opportunity for independence presented by the UN partition plan. They had already formed a government to rule their state when British authority ended. Now their representative, Chaim Weizmann, was asking President Truman to recognize it.

Truman immediately called a meeting with his Secretary of State, Gen. George C. Marshall, and other foreign policy advisers. No decision was made that day, but the next day, May 14, opinion began to swing in favor of granting recognition to the new Jewish state. At 6:15 that evening, a note was handed to Warren Austin, the United States representative to the UN General Assembly in New York. The note instructed Austin to stop arguing in favor of an international trusteeship for Palestine and to read instead a brief statement on behalf of President Truman. This is the statement that Austin read to the General Assembly:

"This government has been informed that a Jewish state has been proclaimed in Palestine, and recognition has been requested by the Provisional Government itself. The United States recognizes the Provisional Government as the *de facto* authority of the new State of Israel."

Recognition of the legitimacy of Israel by the foremost power in the world was bound to infuriate the Arab delegates. "We have been duped!" shouted Dr. Charles Malik of Lebanon to the American representative. Perhaps the Arab diplomats were consoled by the knowledge that armies from Syria, Lebanon, Iraq, Jordan, and Egypt were already crossing Israel's borders, determined to destroy the new state at its inception. For while the time in New York was 6:15 P.M., May 14, in Israel it was 12:15 A.M., May 15.

British rule ended officially at midnight, when most of the Arab armies launched their attack. The Egyptian army hadn't even waited for the midnight deadline; it invaded Israel at sunrise, May 14.

U.S. recognition did much to bolster the morale of the Israelis, but it did not avert their immediate danger. They were faced with a war for survival, and to most foreign observers, their chances seemed exceedingly thin. Although the Arab armies were neither very large nor, with the exception of Jordan's Arab Legion, particularly efficient, they were well-armed. On May 15, the Arabs had more than 150 field guns, a like number of armored cars, 30-40 tanks, and about 55 fighter planes. The Israelis, by contrast, had only rifles, machine guns, and mortars. This disparity in weapons existed because the British had maintained a tight naval blockade of Palestine to prevent arms reaching the Haganah. The British blockade had also kept thousands of Jewish immigrants, most of them survivors of Nazi concentration camps, from entering the country.

Full mobilization of the Jewish population enabled Israel to put about 50,000 men (and some women) into the field. For the most part, their training was as limited as their equipment. But what the Israelis lacked in firepower and experience, they offset by tenacity, an extraordinary ability to improvise, and leadership that was both able and brave. For the Israelis, there was no place to flee to; they had to hold their ground or be destroyed. This was a major source of their strength. By contrast, the Arab forces were divided by political rivalries that prevented the creation of a unified command. Each Arab nation was jealous of the other's territorial ambitions in the area. As a consequence, the Arab armies were almost as wary of each other as they were of the Israelis.

Yet in the first few days it seemed that the Arabs would overrun Israel. By May 20, Syrian forces had captured several northern settlements and were threatening others. On May 19, the Israelis suffered a major disaster when the Arab Legion penetrated the walled Old City of Jerusalem, trapping about 2,500 Jews inside. Fearing a massacre, the Israelis tried desperately to break through the Old City's gates and retake the Jewish quarter, but all their efforts were repulsed. Eventually all of the Old City fell to the Arab Legion, and many Jews were either massacred or taken prisoner.

In the western part of Jerusalem — the new city — Jewish civilians, aided by a small contingent of soldiers, were able to stem the Arab Legion advance. But their position was becoming more precarious day by day. The Legion had cut the road into the city from Israeli-held territory, preventing supplies of food and ammunition from reaching it.

Meanwhile Egyptian armies were advancing into Israel from the south. One column pushed up the coast to within 25 miles of the city of Tel Aviv;

another struck toward Jerusalem, intending to link up with the Arab Legion. (This thrust was motivated more by suspicion of Jordan than any wish to assist it.)

In this dark hour, Israel's prime minister, David Ben-Gurion, made a decision that would rally his country from defeat. Against the advice of his generals, Ben-Gurion ordered that top priority be given to the relief of besieged Jerusalem. Holding Jerusalem was the key to holding the rest of the country, Ben-Gurion maintained; the loss of this symbolic city would be a crushing blow to the morale of Israel's defenders. Ben-Gurion's military leaders argued the reverse; Jerusalem could only be saved if the rest of the country was first secured. Ben-Gurion prevailed, and the Israelis began making strenuous efforts to break the siege.

The chief obstacle was the Arab Legion stronghold of Latrun, dominated by a massive, thick-walled fortress and guns that commanded the road from Tel Aviv to Jerusalem. The Israelis made several frontal attacks on Latrun, but each time were driven back with heavy losses.

Finally the Israelis tried another tactic. Working under cover of darkness, hundreds of recruits — men and women — began building a new road over hills that bypassed Latrun on the south. A rough road was completed after five nights of back-breaking work, and the next day Israeli trucks began to enter the new city of Jerusalem. Written in large letters on the first trucks was a quotation from the Old Testament: "If I forget thee, O Jerusalem, may my right hand forget its cunning." By this time, rations of bread and water in the new city were minimal. Crowds greeted the convoys with almost hysterical joy.

At the end of nearly four weeks of heavy fighting, the Arabs had achieved some successes, but nothing like the "Mongol massacre" they had envisioned. Both sides were exhausted, and welcomed the 30-day truce that was effected by the United Nations Security Council. While the UN strove to find a peaceful solution to the conflict, both the Israelis and the Arabs reinforced their armies (in violation of the truce). The Israelis, however, stood to gain the most. The British blockade had ended on May 15, and Israeli purchases of heavy equipment began to trickle in soon after. Most of the planes, armored cars, and guns were culled from the huge scrapyards of World War II armaments that still littered Europe. Ironically, Israel's first fighter planes were rebuilt German Messerschmitts. Israel was also reinforced by the arrival of many thousands of Jewish refugees who had been lingering in European detention camps.

When both sides rejected the UN's peace proposal, fighting resumed. Now it was the Israelis' turn to take the offensive, and they held it throughout the rest of the war. It was an on-again, off-again war, interrupted by several UN truces, but ultimately the Arab forces were utterly exhausted. One by one, the Arab nations entered into negotiations with Israel for an armistice. By July 20, 1949, 14 months after it began, the first Arab-Israeli conflict was over.

Israel had won its War of Independence and gained in the process one-third more territory than it had at the beginning. (Israel, Jordan, and Egypt divided among them the portion of Palestine that had originally been allotted to an independent Arab state. Palestinian Arabs got nothing.) Yet the cost of victory came high. Israel's dead numbered 6,000, which was a great deal for a nation of only 650,000 people. Despite its grief, Israel faced the future hopefully. Its people had demonstrated courage and an ability to make the most of limited resources. Above all, they had shown a willingness to make sacrifices for their nation's survival.

III

WHO ARE
THE TERRORISTS?

Israel's victory in its War of Independence did not mean that its future was secured. The Arab nations remained implacably hostile to the existence of a Jewish nation in the Middle East and Arab leaders threatened "to drive Israel into the sea." The spirit of revenge pervaded a directive to Egyptian army officers in 1956:

"Every officer must prepare himself and his subordinates for the inevitable struggle with Israel, with the object of realizing our noble aim, namely the annihilation of Israel and her destruction in the shortest possible time and in the most brutal and cruel of battles."

In three subsequent wars fought with Israel (in 1956, 1967, and 1973), Arab arms failed to accomplish their objective. The 1967 war was, in fact, a disaster for the Arabs; they were crushed by the Israelis in a "blitz" (lightning) campaign that lasted just six days. As a consequence, the Israelis occupied and retained territories that had belonged to Egypt, Jordan, and Syria.

Less dangerous to the Israelis than Arab armies, but in many ways more troublesome, was the development of terrorist organizations composed of Palestinian Arabs. All these terrorist groups are branches of the Palestinian Liberation Organization (PLO), which was founded in 1964 and is headed by Yasir Arafat. All are pledged to the destruction of Israel and the establishment of an independent Arab state of Palestine. The oldest and largest of these groups is *Fatah*, which in Arabic means "conquest." Fatah has about 10,000 members who carry out guerrilla raids against settlements within Israel. Later terrorist organizations, like the Popular Front for the Liberation of Palestine (PFLP), extended the war against Israel beyond its borders. Their relatively new techniques include the hijacking of airliners, the indiscriminate slaying of passengers at airports, the selective slaying of political figures considered "soft" on Israel, and other murderous forays.

The PLO claims to represent the more than three million Palestinian Arabs now living in other Arab states, in territories occupied by Israel, and within Israel itself. About 700,000 of them are refugees who fled from Israel during the War of Independence. They live in squalid camps maintained by the United Nations in Arab countries. Only Jordan among the Arab nations has offered to resettle them. (The Palestinians are generally unwanted by the Arab nations, who regard them as burdens.) Most of these refugees, sustained by promises that Israel will be destroyed, still wait for the day when they can return to their former homes. Used as pawns in the conflict between the Arab nations and Israel, they are considerably demoralized. The young are recruited by the PLO and trained in terrorist techniques. PLO units exist within the camps.

What kind of men lead the terrorist organizations? Most of them profess to be disciples of Karl Marx, the theoretician of the Communist movement, and V.I. Lenin, who led the Communist revolution in Russia. Their left-wing sentiments are united to even stronger feelings of Arab nationalism and, sometimes, to Moslem convictions. Generally they live secretly in cities like Beirut or Damascus, but change their quarters frequently. Arafat seldom sleeps in the same house for more than one night, and sometimes less than that. Such precautions are designed to protect him from dissident terrorists as well as Israeli agents. Arafat often visits the refugee camps where he has created the image of a kindly father and a fearless commander.

Dr. George Habash, head of the PFLP, is a Christian Arab, but is even more militant in his opposition to Israel than Arafat and other Moslem leaders. Habash first gained notoriety in 1970 with a series of spectacular hijackings. On September 6, 1970, members of the PFLP hijacked *three* airliners — one Pan American, one TWA, and one Swissair — en route from European airports to New York. Two of the planes were forced to land in Jordan, the other in Egypt. After the passengers and crews were removed, all three planes were blown up. What did Habash hope to accomplish by these acts of piracy and destruction? First, to gain publicity for himself and his movement. Second, to intimidate or coerce all those who might not be in sympathy with his goals.

It wasn't long before Dr. Habash won even bigger headlines for his movement. On May 30, 1972, three members of a Japanese terrorist group known as the Red Army landed at Ben-Gurion airport near Tel Aviv. They had been recruited by the PFLP, which has strong ties with revolutionaries in the Far East. On entering the terminal, the Japanese took automatic weapons from their luggage and began firing indiscriminately at the passengers inside. Before Israeli guards gunned down two of the Japanese and captured the third, 27 men and women were killed and 80 wounded. Most of the victims were Puerto Ricans who had come to Israel to visit the religious shrines.

Ironically, people who commit such atrocities often claim that they are idealists. They say that revolutionary violence is a justifiable means to a good end — the destruction of capitalism and the establishment of a world socialist society. One leader of the PFLP recently told an interviewer, "You must differentiate between the kind of violence used to exploit people and that used in self-defense — legitimate violence. The bullets that I shoot are not the bullets used to exploit or to subdue. They are just the opposite. They will remove exploitation inflicted upon me.

"It is true that innocent people might suffer, might be killed. Why do we do it? Do you think Palestinians love to kill? Of course not. I am committed to killing to save my people, who have been humiliated for more than 25 years. It may take 50 or 100 years of struggle, but even so it is the only solution. The end will come with the establishment of a progressive socialist society throughout the world.

"I should tell you that I am not mad, and I don't live with illusions. I know exactly what our movement can achieve. I know exactly what will be the eventual solution."

Yet some people who have studied the terrorist mentality believe that it is both abnormal and deluded. Albert Parry, author of *Terrorism: From Robespierre to Arafat*, says, "Despite their lofty protestations, many political terrorists are acting out of the disturbances of their minds and souls rather than out of political reasons. If it is possible to explain all human behavior in terms of emotion, so it is logical to ascribe much of terrorism to the influence of emotion upon the terrorists — to postulate that many terrorists are disturbed in extreme ways mentally.

"For their insane violence, blame their families, blame society, if you will. But the true cause is deeper, in a configuration of fear and hatred, in their own innermost drive to do violence. In nonpolitical violence, the dark drive is sheerly criminal. In political terror, it is prettified with programs and slogans."

Dr. David G. Hubbard, a Dallas psychiatrist, believes that hijackers and political terrorists are almost always paranoid (suffering from delusions of persecution) with strong suicidal tendencies. "To this kind of mentality," he says, "death is not the ultimate punishment, it is the ultimate reward."

The Palestinian terrorists have received ample support from many powerful sources. Financial backing comes from Arab governments whose coffers are overflowing with money derived from the sale of oil. In October, 1974, the heads of Arab governments meeting at Rabat, Morocco, voted to give $200 million to the Palestine Liberation Organization which, in turn, supports other terrorist groups. One of the most generous supporters of terrorist operations is Libya's dictator, Col. Muammar Qadaffi. As a reward for the murder of Israeli athletes at the Olympic games in Munich, Qaddafi presented Arafat with a bonus of five million dollars for the Black September group. Arms and forged passports flow into guerrilla bases from practically every Arab country. Chief supplier of arms is the Soviet Union; it sells automatic weapons, mortars, anti-tank and surface-to-air missiles to PLO groups.

When the terrorist organizations first began hijacking airplanes as part of their war against Israel, the Israeli government reluctantly gave in to their demands. Soon after, however, the Israelis took tough measures to prevent or discourage further attempts at blackmail. Specially-trained security guards were assigned to protect El Al Israel planes and airport facilities. They have since foiled several attempts to hijack or blow up airliners. The government adopted a firm policy of refusing to negotiate with terrorists for release of Israeli hostages. Finally, the Israelis began a determined campaign of fighting terror with terror. Their fighter planes have retaliated for acts of Arab terrorism by bombing and strafing guerrilla bases. Commando units have landed on the coast of Lebanon and executed guerrilla leaders. Terrorists have been slain by Israeli agents in cities from western Europe to the Middle East.

The government has relented from its policy of not negotiating with terrorists on only two occasions in recent years. The first occurred on May 15, 1974, when three Palestinian guerrillas invaded a school in the Israeli village of Ma'alot and held 85 teenage children as hostages. They demanded the release of 10 prisoners serving life sentences in Israeli jails on charges of murder and sabotage. One of the prisoners specified was Kozo Okamato, the Japanese terrorist who had participated in the slaughter of 27 passengers at Ben-Gurion airport in 1972. "You had better hurry," the guerrillas warned, "or at six o'clock you are going to get 85 dead bodies." The Israeli cabinet met in an emergency session and decided that, because of the youthfulness of the hostages, it would yield to the terrorists' demands.

As the terrorists' deadline approached, however, they began to make new demands. They wanted two additional prisoners released, and insisted on taking half of their hostages with them to Damascus. The Israelis pleaded for more time to deal with these demands, but the Arabs refused. Finally, in a desperate attempt to save the children, Israeli snipers opened fire on the terrorists while other soldiers stormed the school building. One of the Arabs was killed immediately, but the two others fired their Russian submachine guns pointblank at the children. When the carnage ended, 17 students were dead, and scores wounded. Five of the wounded died afterward in hospitals. The next day, Israeli jets retaliated with strikes against Palestinian refugee camps and guerrilla bases in Lebanon. The raids took about 50 lives and left more than 200 wounded.

The second occasion on which the Israelis agreed to negotiate with terrorists took place in the summer of 1976 under equally terrifying circumstances. On Sunday, June 27, agents of the PFLP hijacked a French airliner with more than

250 passengers aboard and forced it to land at Entebbe, Uganda. They demanded the release of 53 "freedom fighters" in exchange for the passengers, many of whom were Israelis. The terrorists soon released all but their Israeli hostages. These they threatened to kill unless their demands were met.

If the government of Israel capitulated, the hostages would be saved, but almost certainly more terrorist acts would threaten the nation's existence. If the government did not capitulate, 103 Israeli citizens faced death. This was the dilemma posed by the hijacking of Flight 139 from Tel Aviv on Sunday, June 27, 1976.

IV

THE HIJACKING
OF FLIGHT 139

Sunday, June 27, 1976

Flight 139, a weekly Air France shuttle from Tel Aviv to Paris, lifted off the runway at Ben-Gurion Airport at approximately 8:50 A.M., Sunday, June 27. At the controls of the twin-engined jet was Captain Michel Bacos, a 52-year-old veteran pilot. All the passengers had undergone intensive security checks at the airport. Luggage and handbags had been painstakingly examined, and each passenger required to pass through electronic metal detectors. In some instances, passengers were frisked by security guards. Of the 245 travelers who boarded Flight 139, about half were French citizens who had been visiting the Holy Land. One-third were Israeli citizens who were heading for vacations in Europe or America. A number of passengers were citizens of both France and Israel, and a smattering came from other countries.

Most of ths Israeli passengers were businessmen or professionals who could afford the expensive air fare and travel tax. Among them were Uzi Davidson, a factory manager, his wife, Sarah, and their two sons, Ron, 16, and Benjamin, 13; Ilan Hartuv, an economist who was planning to spend a month's vacation in France and Spain; his 75-year-old mother, Mrs. Dora Bloch, who was en route to New York to attend the wedding of a younger son; Moshe Peretz, a 26-year-old medical student; and Michal Warshavsky, a 15-year-old high school girl from Jerusalem who was traveling alone to visit relatives in Paris.

At about the same time that these passengers were undergoing security checks at Ben-Gurion Airport, four travelers from Bahrain, an island country close to Arabia in the Persian Gulf, were arriving at Athens Airport in Greece. At 6:17 A.M., they disembarked from Singapore Airlines Flight 763 and entered the airport lounge. All were traveling under fictitious names. All were due to board Air France Flight 139 when it arrived at Athens for a scheduled stop before noon. All were carrying hand luggage containing pistols and grenades.

Two of them were male Palestinian Arabs in their 20's wearing sport shirts and slacks. Israeli intelligence has since identified one as Jayel Naji al-Arjam, a member of the PFLP who was known to have recruited agents for the organization among South American revolutionaries. The other Palestinian has not been identified, but it is assumed that he too was a member of the PFLP. The other two arrivals from Bahrain were a man and a woman, both German, both in their 20's. The man was fair-haired, husky, and tall. He wore a brown suit and a green shirt. Israeli intelligence has identified him as Wilfried Böse, a member of an anarchist group known as the Baader-Meinhoff gang, which has committed numerous terrorist acts in West Germany. The woman was wearing a blue denim skirt, a light blue blouse, and flat-heeled shoes. Israeli intelligence believes that she was Gabriele Kroche-Tiedemann. She was part of a team that had kidnapped nearly a dozen Arab oil ministers from their Viennna headquarters in December, 1975, demanding that their governments declare war against Israel. According to one Israeli intelligence chief, "The Popular Front for the Liberation of Palestine has the closest relations with undergrounds and extreme organizations in the world. The basis for collaboration is both ideological and practical. They have the common ideology of fighting against 'imperialism and Zionism,' and in practice they can assist one another. This collaboration among various terrorist groups hasn't yet resulted in an international terrorist organization, but it does create the danger of such an organization."

When Flight 139 landed at Athens Airport, 38 passengers disembarked and more than 40 new passengers, including the four terrorists, got on. Unfortunately, security procedures at the airport were quite lax; the hand luggage carried by the new passengers was not even examined. Once inside the plane, the four terrorists split up. The Arabs took seats in the economy class section at the rear. The Germans entered the first-class section up front. At least one of the passengers, Dora Bloch, felt some concern about the presence of the two Arabs among them. She whispered to her son that they were carrying cases large enough to contain concealed weapons. It made her nervous, she said, but her son did not share her anxiety.

At 12:25 P.M., Flight 139 took off for Paris. The plane climbed through a thin layer of smog and then banked westward over the Gulf of Corinth. Nearly ten minutes later, when the "Fasten Seat Belts" signs were still lighted, the passengers were startled by a woman's scream. Moshe Peretz, the medical student, thought that someone had fainted. Ron Davidson wrote down his own impressions of that moment:

"When I heard a woman scream, I thought she must be air sick. But after a few seconds, more and more women started screaming, and when two men [the Arab terrorists] rushed to the first-class compartment, I knew that something irregular was happening.

"Father, who was just as puzzled as the rest of us, told us to get our heads down and crouch as low as we could into our seats. Mother said we were being hijacked, but I knew she was being too melodramatic. There couldn't be a hijacking on a French plane. I asked myself what it could all be about. Of course — security officers were checking out the plane, to see how the crew would react in such an emergency."

In the first-class section, the Germans had sprung to their feet, each brandishing a pistol in one hand and a grenade in the other. While the German woman trained her gun on the terrified stewardesses, the man moved toward the pilot's cabin. Behind the insulated door, Captain Bacos had heard the screams and the commotion in the first-class compartment.

"First, I thought there was a fire on board," he said later. "Then the chief engineer opened the door and found himself nose to nose with the German hijacker."

Böse pushed inside the cabin and grabbed the microphone of the plane's public address system. Speaking in English, but with a heavy German accent, he told the passengers, "My name is Ahmed el-Kubesi of the Gaza Strip, Che Guevera commando unit of the Popular Front for the Liberation of Palestine. [The name el-Kubesi is believed to be that of a slain guerrilla who is regarded as a martyr by the Palestinians.] If you raise your hands above your heads and don't move, no one will be hurt."

Böse told the passengers that they were being hijacked in the name of "Arab and world revolution," and denounced the Israelis at length as oppressors of the Palestinian people. His oration concluded, Böse ordered Captain Bacos to fly the plane to Benghazi, Libya, where it would be refueled.

To simplify the process of guarding and searching the passengers, the hijackers ordered everyone in the first-class compartment to move back to the economy class section. Some of these passengers were forced to sit in the aisle with their hands behind their heads. One by one the passengers were called forward to be searched for weapons. The hijackers showed some sensitivity for their victims' feelings. Women were frisked by Gabriele Kroche-Teidemann, the men by the two Arabs. To Moshe Peretz, it appeared that the searches became more superficial as time went on. Nevertheless, the process took almost three hours.

Once the passengers recovered from their initial shock at being hijacked, the atmosphere on the plane became less tense. Though forbidden to talk, the passengers whispered to each other, usually speculating about where they would be taken. Some read books and newspapers, while mothers, as always, tended to their childrens' needs. The stewardesses began serving cold drinks as though nothing had happened. Indeed, it appeared to the passengers that the most nervous people on the plane were the hijackers. Uzi Davidson later recalled, "The terrorists themselves were terrified. They were so nervous that I thought they might start shooting because of it."

About three o'clock in the afternoon, the passengers spotted a coastline, arid soil, and then an airfield. Some of the passengers guessed correctly that it was Benghazi Airport in Libya. The plane circled the airport several times before coming down to a bumpy landing. Böse informed the passengers "officially" that they were in Benghazi and told them that the plane would take off again as soon as it was refueled.

Strangely, the plane remained on the runway at Benghazi for more than six hours. For the Israeli passengers especially, the situation did not seem hopeful. As one woman recalled, "We knew — my neighbors and I — that our 'visit' to an Arab country dedicated to the destruction of Israel was not good news. This was certainly not a safe haven for us. An hour passed, and another hour, and we sat there in silence, heavy with foreboding."

At Benghazi, the terrorists tied cans that appeared to have fuses to the exit doors. The passengers were told that these cans contained explosives and would blow up in case anyone tried to open a door. To Moshe Peretz, the cans didn't seem very lethal, and he was right. Later, at Entebbe, the cans were opened. They contained nothing more dangerous than candied dates, which the hijackers laughingly handed out to their hostages.

The monotony of staring at a desert landscape was broken about 5 P.M. when a woman passenger, Mrs. Pat Heyman, became ill and was taken off the plane. An English citizen who made her home in Israel, Mrs. Heyman was pregnant. Because of her condition, she was released by the hijackers. Undoubtedly, her British passport helped. Mrs. Heyman arrived the next day in London where she was interrogated by Scotland Yard's anti-terrorist unit. Her information about the hijacking was then relayed to Israeli intelligence.

After Mrs. Heyman was removed from the plane, the hijackers began confiscating the passengers' passports and all other documents containing identification. They threatened "severe punishment" for anyone who didn't comply. Later the stewardesses served a cold dinner that featured a Jewish delicacy, gefilte fish. Akiva Laxer, a 30-year-old lawyer from Tel Aviv, was quietly amused to find himself eating gefilte fish in Arab Libya.

The plane had been on the runway for several hours when Böse once again spoke to the passengers over the public address system. He told them that he regretted the discomfort caused them by the long delay, but assured them that the plane would soon take off. He thanked them for their "cooperation," and said he hoped it would continue for the rest of the journey. At approximately 9:35, the plane took off for what Böse said would be its "last destination." By this time, the atmosphere on the plane was relaxed, and everyone was talking freely. The passengers wondered aloud about their destination. Would it be Damascus? Beirut? Tel Aviv? Paris? The wildest guesses were China and India. No one suggested the possibility of a place as obscure as Uganda.

Meanwhile, the plane's destination had become a matter of concern to other people. Flight 139 was scheduled to land at the Charles de Gaulle Airport near Paris at 1:35 that afternoon, and many relatives and friends of the passengers were on hand to meet it. Before long, the word "DELAYED" appeared next to the flight's arrival time, but no further information was available. Later a voice repeated over the loudspeaker system, "Attention, please. Air France apologizes for the delay in the arrival of Flight 139. Those awaiting Flight 139 will please come to the central Air France office."

In Tel Aviv, the disappearance of Flight 139 was monitored by an Israeli intelligence unit that, by means of powerful electronic devices, keeps track of all planes flying to and from Israel. When contact with Flight 139 was lost, this unit forwarded a message to Transport Minister Gad Yaacobi, who was then in the middle of a cabinet meeting in Jerusalem. The message said, "Flight 139 with a very large number of Israelis aboard has either crashed or been hijacked. The missing Air France aircraft left Ben-Gurion Airport shortly after nine this morning."

Yaacobi passed the message to Prime Minister Rabin and other members of the cabinet. Soon more messages began arriving, including one that "an unknown number of Arabs are believed to have transferred to Flight 139 from a Singapore Airlines flight at Athens." Before long, it was apparent that Flight 139 had been hijacked, and a crisis team of six cabinet ministers headed by Rabin was formed to deal with the situation. According to Defense Minister Shimon Peres, a member of the team, "Our first reaction was that we should not surrender to terrorist demands. And since this was an Air France plane, we should hold the French government responsible for the fate of the passengers."

At this time, French President Valery Giscard d'Estaing was in Puerto Rico, attending an economic conference with U.S. President Gerald Ford and other heads of state. Informed of the hijacking, d'Estaing not only accepted full responsibility for the airliner, but took a hard line toward the terrorists. France, he said, would make no deal that did not include the release of *all* hostages, not just French citizens.

According to *The Jerusalem Post,* France's ambassador to Libya learned that Flight 139 was refueling at Benghazi and attempted, without success, to have the passengers freed. This would account for the long delay before the hijacked airliner took off for its "last destination."

Israel's leaders did not know where the plane was heading from Libya, but they did not rule out the possibility that it might return to Ben-Gurion Airport. They recalled that in May, 1972, four Arab terrorists had hijacked a Belgian Sabena airliner at Vienna and forced the pilot to fly it to Tel Aviv. There the hijackers demanded that Israel free a number of Arab guerrillas in its jails. On that occasion, Israeli security guards disguised as mechanics and ground attendants opened fire on the terrorists, killing two and capturing the others. (One passenger was also killed.) So on the afternoon of June 27, the Israelis set up a command post at Ben-Gurion Airport in case Flight 139 should return there.

About midnight, Gen. Mordechai Gur, Chief of Staff of the Israeli Defense Forces, called Defense Minister Peres with the latest information on the Air France liner. Israeli intelligence, Gur said, believed that the plane was then flying over Khartoum in the Sudan, its destination unknown. Khartoum is about half-way between Benghazi and Entebbe, but only a few hours flying time from Israel. Peres decided to go out to the airport himself to keep on top of the situation.

"Around three o'clock in the morning," Peres recalled, "we received information that the plane was circling around Entebbe Airport in Uganda. According to our calculations, it was low on fuel and would have to land there. Finally we learned that Entebbe had, in fact, received the plane."

V

IDI AMIN MAKES
HIS ENTRANCE

Monday, June 28, 1976

When the hijacked airliner finally landed at Entebbe Airport, the passengers felt relieved, and most were optimistic that they would soon be freed. "Once again it was the German terrorist [Böse] who raised our hopes," Mrs. Davidson remembered. " 'We have arrived at Entebbe, Uganda, where the Ugandan people will help you and us,' he said. He went on talking in a soothing voice, giving us the feeling that it was all over and we were about to be released. We all clapped our hands when he finished his announcement, and some even shed tears of joy."

Nevertheless the passengers were not allowed off the plane, nor could they see what was happening outside. On Böse's orders, all window shades had been drawn before the landing. At dawn some of the passengers opened the shades slightly and peeked out. Moshe Peretz, who was keeping a diary, noted that the plane was parked on a runway beside "a gigantic lake," and that Ugandan soldiers were surrounding the airliner. Entebbe Airport is, in fact, situated on the northwestern shore of Lake Victoria, which is the largest in Africa. Kampala, the capital city of Uganda, is about 20 miles from the airport.

From time to time, Böse made some announcements that were intended to be reassuring. The passengers were told that President Idi Amin of Uganda would be arriving soon to take charge of the negotiations . . . there was nothing to worry about. At nine o'clock, the rear door of the plane was opened and Moshe Peretz could see the tall, hulking figure of Idi Amin, Uganda's dictator. A former army heavyweight boxing champion, Amin is six feet, four inches tall, and weighs 280 pounds. Sometimes clownish in his behavior, he has been nicknamed "Big Daddy" by his political detractors. Amin was in earnest conversation with three other men. These were Arab terrorists who had been waiting at the airport for the hijacked plane to arrive. They were heavily armed with Russian Kalachnikov automatic rifles, which have become status symbols to the guerrilla movement.

Soon Böse told the passengers that "the main danger is past." Once again he indulged in some political oratory, denouncing France for selling fighter planes to Israel and calling Israel a "fascist" state that engaged in genocide against Palestinian Arabs. He and his companions, he said, were *not* planning to murder the passengers. "I want to be human and I don't want to kill you," he added. "But I am very tired and a little confused. Now you have an inkling of a lunatic's mind at work."

The hijackers then descended briefly to the runway where they were warmly embraced by the three terrorists who had been waiting for them. The passengers were allowed to get up and walk around inside the plane.

About noon, Amin's talks with the Arab terrorists ended. The plane's engines started again and the airliner taxied up to the entrance of a rundown passenger terminal building. This building was part of the old airport at Entebbe that had fallen into disuse since new facilities were built nearby. Finally the doors of the plane were opened and the passengers told that they could leave. "The bad dream is over," Böse told them. Many of the passengers hugged and kissed each other, certain that that their ordeal had ended and that they were now free. But as they walked down the stairs to the ground, they were startled by the sight of Ugandan soldiers lined up on either side of the path to the terminal building. The soldiers kept their rifles pointed at the passengers.

"That seemed very strange," recalled Gabriella Rubenstein, a psychologist from Jerusalem. "We thought we were free. Then we saw the terrorist reinforcements again greet the hijackers, and the real bad news followed."

As soon as the passengers had entered the terminal, Böse picked up a loudspeaker and announced, "I want to remind you that you are still under our control."

It was now 24 hours since Flight 139 had been hijacked. In Israel, the public took the news calmly. It was, after all, a French plane and the government of France had assumed responsibility for the passengers' safety. So far the hijackers had not issued any demands, but Defense Minister Peres and high-ranking army officers were already exploring the possibility of a military rescue mission. At the moment, however, no feasible plan for such a long-range operation existed.

"We did not have any idea how to save the lives of the passengers," Peres remembered. "My first thought was, if we didn't have a plan, either because we lacked information or time, our plan must be to gain time. By gaining time, we would be able to prepare something."

Prior to 1972, Israel had maintained a military cadre in Uganda to train that country's armed forces. Peres called in a number of the officers who had served there and asked them for an assessment of Idi Amin. All of them agreed that the Ugandan dictator might unwittingly become a partner in Israel's plan to gain time. Amin, they said, was a man who thoroughly enjoyed being the center of attention. He would undoubtedly prolong the drama that was unfolding at Entebbe as much as possible to remain in the spotlight. As Peres said, "He is like a child in the middle of a room full of guests. The more attention he gets, the more he wishes to remain."

Peres believed that the hijackers themselves would abet Israel's objective of gaining time. Negotiations for an exchange of prisoners would be complicated by the distance from Entebbe; they would undoubtedly require several days. In the meantime, the hostages would be safe, and Israel's Defense Forces could develop a military option.

Afterward Peres asked Col. Baruch Bar-Lev (ret.), a former chief of the Israeli training force in Uganda, to telephone Amin. It was hoped that Bar-Lev, who had once been quite close to the Ugandan dictator, might persuade him to effect the release of the hostages. In any event, Peres wanted Bar-Lev to maintain daily contact with Amin. Useful information might be obtained, and valuable time might be won to prepare a military operation.

Meanwhile the hostages at Entebbe were getting acquainted with their new surroundings. The main passenger lounge of the old terminal was a huge room, now grimy and dusty after years of disuse. Ugandan civilians were working at a number of tasks: bringing in additional chairs, repairing the overhead fans, and making the toilets serviceable. The hostages soon broke up into small groups of friends and relatives and tried to make themselves as comfortable as possible. The hijackers, now armed with automatic weapons provided by their reinforcements, stood on guard outside the terminal's entrance. Ugandan soldiers were posted all around the building at a distance of about 20 yards. To the hostages, it appeared that there was complete cooperation between the terrorists and the soldiers. Later Mrs. Jan Almogs, an Israeli who lives in a farm community, recalled, "The Ugandan troops outnumbered the hijackers perhaps 20 to one. Had they wanted to overcome them, there would have been no problem whatever. They had the weaponry and the manpower to do it in a second. But they didn't. They took orders from the hijackers, and there was no question at any point that they were collaborating with them."

Shortly after 2 P.M., pots of hot curry and rice were brought in for the hostages' lunch. Michel Cojot, a French management consultant who served as an interpreter for his compatriots, observed further evidence of Uganda's collusion in the hijacking. When he asked the airport manager for more plates for the hostages, he jokingly remarked, "It must be hard for you to look after 263 unexpected guests." The manager replied, "Oh, but I *was* expecting you."

Afterwards the hostages were photographed by Ugandan television cameramen and informed that they would soon be visited by President Amin. About five o'clock, a helicopter was heard circling overhead, presaging the dictator's arrival. A few minutes later, Amin entered the terminal. He was wearing a paratrooper's uniform with Israeli paratrooper wings pinned to his chest, and a green beret.

"For those of you who don't know me," he announced to the hostages, "I am Field Marshal Dr. Idi Amin Dada." Those who did know Amin's background were aware that his titles — field marshal and doctor of philosophy — were self-bestowed and fraudulent. A career army officer who rose from the enlisted ranks, Amin never had any formal education, "not even a nursery school certificate," he once admitted. "But sometimes I know more than Ph. D's because as a military man I know how to act."

In January, 1971, Amin led a military coup that overthrew the government of President Milton Obote, who had been his benefactor and colleague. Soon after taking power, Amin ordered the expulsion from Uganda of its 80,000 Indian and Pakistani residents, who had largely controlled the country's economy. He also began a reign of terror against his political and tribal enemies. A recent report of the International Commission of Jurists estimated that tens of thousands of them have been murdered. Denis Hills, a British author who resided in Uganda, wrote in 1975, "For several months, soldiers of the northern Langi and Acholi tribes were shot, stabbed and clubbed to death in barracks throughout the country. The killings . . . were no secret. The dead were thrown 'like sacks of *posho*' [maize porridge] into the Nile, into swamps, and into Lake Victoria. Many people saw them."

Under President Obote, Uganda had appealed to Israel for military assistance and cooperation. Israel responded by sending a military mission to Uganda to train and supply its armed forces. Idi Amin was especially enthusiastic about the Israeli presence in Uganda. He made several trips to Israel and had high praise for its military proficiency. Israel awarded him paratrooper wings even though he never earned them by jumping from a plane.

But in 1972, Amin turned against his Israeli benefactors. He had asked Israel for a number of fighter planes and pilots to help him invade Tanzania, Uganda's neighbor to the south. When Israel refused, Amin became furious and expelled its military mission. Soon he embraced the cause of the Palestinian Arabs, and vowed to support their struggle against "Zionism and imperialism." He invited PLO guerrillas to train in Uganda and to serve as his personal bodyguard. When Black September terrorists murdered Israeli Olympic athletes, Amin applauded their deed. He has since praised Adolf Hitler as a great man, and on one occasion announced his intention of building a monument to the Nazi dictator in Kampala. Ironically, Amin's mother was a devout Moslem who taught him that the Israelis were a sacred people, descended from the ancient Hebrews of the Old Testament.

Despite his record, when Amin spoke to the hostages at Entebbe he sounded quite protective.

Though he talked at length of the justness of the Palestinian cause, he ended on a reassuring note. "You are innocent people," he said, "and I will take care of you. I will see to it that you are released." Then, swelling out his chest and grinning broadly, he declared emphatically, "I am good to you."

A number of hostages applauded him, convinced that he was sincere. Others, however, were quite skeptical. "He tried to give us the impression," Mrs. Almogs said, "that he was playing the role of middle man, that he was caught between the hijackers and the governments involved, and that he was trying to negotiate for our lives. But we knew very well that he was part of it all or we would not have been there in the first place."

Among the hostages who remained in good spirits and tried to raise the morale of others was Pasco Cohen, a 52-year-old Israeli who bore the tattoo mark of a Nazi concentration camp on his arm. Cohen told the hostages, "You are lucky to be traveling with me. I'm a specialist at getting out of the most dangerous places. I was one of the few survivors of the Holocaust [the slaughter of six million Jews in Nazi death camps during World War II]. I've taken part in all of Israel's wars and I've faced death many times." The Israelis would have occasion to remember his words later that week.

The hostages' dinner that night consisted of meat, potatoes, rice, and dwarf bananas. Afterwards, a Ugandan doctor gave each of them two antimalaria pills. Near midnight, the hostages decided to try to get some sleep. Moshe Peretz described the scene in his diary:

"Everybody lies down on the filthy floor. It's very hot and there is a veritable symphony of snores. People shout at one another to keep quiet. It's like a summer camp of military cadets."

During the night, the lights in the terminal were kept on. The hostages were guarded by the three terrorists who had met their plane at Entebbe. The hijackers had been given the night off to catch up on their sleep.

VI

THE TERRORISTS' DEMANDS

Tuesday, June 29, 1976

On Tuesday, the terrorists at Entebbe were reinforced by the arrival of three additional members of the PFLP, including one whom Israeli intelligence later identified as a leading figure in the organization's European operations. This man was Antonio Bouvier, a South American revolutionary and an associate of "Carlos," a notorious international terrorist who is wanted by the police of a dozen Western nations. Israeli intelligence believes that Bouvier arrived from Somalia, an east African nation whose population is predominantly Moslem. Israeli intelligence also believes that the man who planned the hijacking of Flight 139 was based at this time in Somalia, where he conducted the PFLP's negotiations with Israel. This man was Wadia Hadad, second

43

only to Dr. Habash in the organization's hierarchy. It was Hadad who conceived the idea of hijacking airliners as an instrument of terror against Israel, and later recruited international terrorists to abet his activities.

At about the same time that Bouvier arrived at Entebbe, the PFLP communicated its demands to Israel. The chain of communications was quite circuitous. From Somalia, Hadad contacted the Somalian ambassador to Uganda. The Somalian ambassador relayed Hadad's demands to Idi Amin and the terrorists at Entebbe. They in turn relayed them to a French diplomat in Uganda who forwarded them to the French Foreign Ministry in Paris. The Foreign Ministry conveyed them to the Israeli ambassador who then communicated them to his government in Israel. The process was reversed when the Israeli government responded to Hadad.

The PFLP's price for its hostages was the release of 53 convicted terrorists in four countries. Forty of them were held in Israel, six in West Germany, five in Kenya, and one each in Switzerland and France. (Hadad assumed that Israel would negotiate for the release of the terrorists held by other nations.) Unless the government of Israel responded affirmatively to these demands by noon on Thursday, the terrorists would blow up the terminal in which the hostages were being held.

The list of prisoners submitted to Israel included some of the most notorious criminals in its jails. One of them was Kozo Akamoto, the Japanese who participated in the machine-gunning of passengers at Ben-Gurion Airport in 1972. Akamoto had been sentenced to life imprisonment. Another was Archbishop Hilarion Capucci, patriarch of the Greek Catholic Church in Jerusalem, who was arrested in 1974 for smuggling weapons to Palestinian terrorists operating within Israel. Capucci had been sentenced to 12 years in prison.

The five prisoners held by Kenya were of more than passing interest to Idi Amin. On January 18, 1976, three Palestinian terrorists armed with Soviet missiles were poised to shoot down an El Al Israel airliner as it was coming in to land at Nairobi Airport in Kenya. Before they could fire their missiles, they were caught by Kenyan security agents. Questioning revealed that the missiles had been supplied by Idi Amin. On January 21, two more terrorists arrived in Nairobi to find out what had happened to their colleagues. They were also arrested by Kenyan security agents and charged with complicity in the plot. All five were now languishing in jail. The PFLP threatened that Kenya would be subjected to "terrible" reprisal actions unless they were set free.

That day, Prime Minister Rabin called a meeting of his cabinet to discuss the PFLP's demands. The ministers were loathe to surrender to Hadad's blackmail. As Transport Minister Yaacobi said, "If we accept the hijackers' condi-

45

tions, the Palestinians will escalate their terror and no Israeli leaving the country will be safe."

Rabin then asked Gen. Gur the question that was on everyone's minds: "Do we have a military option?" Gur had to admit that at this time he did not have a feasible military plan. Gur explained that Lockheed C-130 transport planes, which Israel possessed, were capable of delivering a substantial force of commandos with their equipment to Entebbe. But what would happen once they landed? His primary concern was the vulnerability of the hostages. Unless his commandos could get inside the terminal within seconds, the hostages were certain to be slaughtered. To guarantee the safety of the hostages, he had to have accurate information about the forces guarding Entebbe. How many Ugandan troops were at the airport? Where were they located? What kind of weapons did they have? Gur also needed precise information about the layout of the airfield, and particularly the terminal in which the hostages were being held. Gur did not have such information, and without it he could not produce an operational plan.

As a consequence, the cabinet decided to pursue two parallel courses of action. One called for Israel's formidable intelligence network to learn everything it could about Entebbe so that the Defense Force could assess all the risks of a military operation. The other called for keeping up the appearance of a willingness to negotiate. To that end, Col. Bar-Lev was instructed to call Idi

Amin and offer to fly to Entebbe to expedite negotiations. A portion of Bar-Lev's conversation with Amin follows:

Bar-Lev: "My friend, you have a great opportunity to go down in history as a great peacemaker. . . ."

Amin: "I want you to know that you are my friend for all time . . . . I told the American journalists that Col. Bar-Lev is my friend. I shall be pleased to see you, because I know you well. I'm prepared to make peace between the Israelis and the Arabs. I want you to tell this to your government. . . ."

Bar-Lev: "Can you stop them [the PFLP] from killing until I arrive?"

Amin: "I can do something if your government accepts their demands immediately. . . ."

Bar-Lev: "Very well, sir, I'll call you back later."

Amin: "You can call me whenever you like. I'm waiting . . . I want to save these people."

While the government was keeping open its line to Kampala, military leaders continued to work on plans for a rescue operation. Everything depended on getting reliable intelligence. Kenyans who were secret agents of Israel began moving across the border into Uganda. Soon they would infiltrate the airport at Entebbe and the capital of Kampala. Israeli intelligence officers wearing business suits flew down to Nairobi, Kenya, on various missions. Later in the week, two of them rented planes at Nairobi Airport and

47

flew over Entebbe, photographing the site thoroughly. The planes were not detected.

At Entebbe, Tuesday morning began uneventfully for the hostages. Ugandan waiters carried in coffee, tea, and rolls for their breakfast, and the French airline stewardesses helped with the serving. Afterwards the hostages tried to pass the time as best they could. Mrs. Davidson's group made a checkerboard from a large sheet of paper and used bottle tops as checkers. Another member of the group found a pack of cards and started a game. Some of the hostages had transistor radios and listened intently to news broadcasts from Radio Kampala. Later they heard a report that the government of Israel had reaffirmed its opposition to dealing with terrorists. The hostages began to show signs of anxiety. The decision of the terrorists to permit women and children to relax on the lawn outside the terminal did little to alleviate the mood of gloom.

In the afternoon, the terrorists decided to acquaint the hostages with their demands. The fact that 40 of the 53 prisoners whom the terrorists wanted released were held by Israel disturbed the Israeli hostages. They doubted that their government would ever consent to free such a large number. In his diary, Moshe Peretz predicted — correctly — that the terrorists would soon release "all the passengers, with the exception of the Israelis."

That evening, the worst fears of the Israeli hostages began to materialize. Böse announced that, to relieve the overcrowding in the main passenger lounge, the hostages would be split up into two groups. All those whose names he would call were to move to an adjoining room. Böse emphasized that there was no significance in the way that the hostages were being separated. A French woman later recalled the scene:

"Just before dinner, he began to read out the names. We soon realized that the names were all Hebrew, and that he was calling out the Israelis. Each had to pick up his or her belongings and walk into another room. Some of them wept. We felt just as miserable as they left us."

For the Israelis, the separation process had frightening implications. They were reminded of the experience of Jewish prisoners in Nazi death camps. After being separated from non-Jewish prisoners, the Jews were marched off to gas chambers to be executed. An elderly Israeli woman, who had been in a Nazi concentration camp, felt herself thrust back more than 30 years. "Suddenly," she recalled later, "I heard Germans giving orders, pointing their guns at us, and imagined again the shuffling lines of prisoners and heard the harsh cry: *'Jews to the right!'* I wondered, what good is Israel if this can happen today?"

Michal Warshavsky, the 15-year-old high school girl from Jerusalem, saw another analogy with Nazi concentration camps. She remembered that the entrance to the adjoining room had been partially boarded up so that the Israelis had to duck low to get through. "It was a deliberate attempt on the part of the terrorists to humiliate us," she said. "Later they asked us to write our names on pieces of tape and stick them on our personal belongings, which they were taking away. I was so nervous I could not write my name. At that moment I understood — all the Israelis understood — that the airliner was hijacked because of us. I thought, maybe the French people will go home tomorrow, but the Israelis, never."

The terrorists had placed a number of cardboard boxes around the room and warned the hostages that they were filled with explosives. If the boxes were even touched, the terrorists said, they would blow up. At first the hostages were quite frightened, but later they discovered that these boxes were no more lethal than the cans of dates that had been attached to the doors of their plane. After a while, the hostages hung their clothes on them.

Moshe Peretz concluded his diary for Tuesday on a somber note: "While we are getting organized, one of the hostages goes up to a terrorist and asks for a cushion for his baby. The terrorist strikes him violently with the butt of his revolver. Our second night in Uganda."

VII

THE PRESSURE ON ISRAEL MOUNTS

Wednesday, June 30, 1976

The sound of a helicopter circling over the terminal on Wednesday morning once again heralded a visit from Idi Amin. This time the Ugandan president was wearing a Tyrolean hunting outfit with a feather stuck in his hat. He was greeted quite coolly when he entered the room where the Israelis were being held. Undaunted, Amin said "Shalom" — the Hebrew greeting meaning "Peace" — over and over until at last he was applauded. He promised to give the Israelis mattresses and blankets, but said nothing reassuring about their fate. The terrorists had nothing against them personally, he declared; it was the "fascist government" of Israel that had provoked the hijacking. If the government did not give in to the guerrillas' demands, then it did not

Ben-Gurion Airport at Tel Aviv, Israel.

Type of airliner hijacked by terrorists.

Old passenger terminal and control tower (left) at

Israeli Government Press Office

Israeli commandos practice for airborne mission.

54

Israeli Government Press Office

Entebbe Airport, Uganda.

Israeli Government Press Office

Model of terminal built by Israelis.

Alain Taieb/Sygma

Israeli commandos training for night raids.

Israeli Government Press Office

Rescue plane lands at Ben-Gurion Airport.

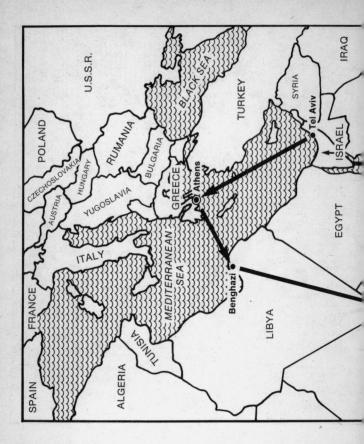

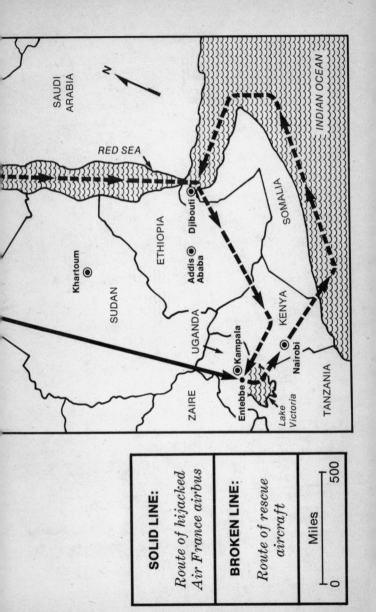

SOLID LINE:
Route of hijacked Air France airbus

BROKEN LINE:
Route of rescue aircraft

Miles
0 — 500

Israeli Government Press Office

Capt. Michel Bacos, pilot of hijacked airliner, leaves Israeli rescue plane at Tel Aviv.

Israeli Government Press Office

Michal Warshavsky, 15-year-old Israeli hostage, greeted tearfully by her mother after rescue.

Israeli Government Press Office

Another emotional scene as hostages return to Ben-Gurion Airport after ordeal at Entebbe.

Photo AFP from Pictorial

Prime Minister Yitzhak Rabin of Israel approved rescue mission to Entebbe despite risks.

The Jerusalem Post

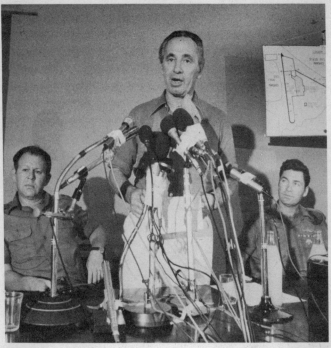

Defense Minister Shimon Peres talks to diplomats and newsmen after successful Israeli raid. Seated at left is Gen. Mordechai Gur, Israel's Chief of Staff. Seated at right is Gen. Dan Shomron, who planned and led commando raid at Entebbe.

Sygma

*Idi Amin, 280-pound dictator of Uganda, is called
"Big Daddy" by his critics. Amin still wears Israeli
paratrooper wings on his uniforms.*

Genevieve CHAUVEL/Sygma

Yasir Arafat, head of the terrorist Palestine Liberation Organization, poses with some of his guerrillas. Armed with Soviet weapons, guerrillas attack Israeli towns and villages.

care about the fate of its citizens. One Israeli asked Amin why his soldiers had made no effort to overpower the terrorists and release the hostages. Amin replied that if his soldiers were to try it, the terrorists would blow up the building instantly. (Amin gave the same explanation to Col. Bar-Lev later that day. "The terrorists have surrounded the hostages and they say they can blow them all up, and the Ugandan troops too.")

In the meantime, the non-Israeli hostages, most of whom were French, had received some encouraging news. The terrorists had decided to release 47 of them that day. This group consisted mainly of invalids, elderly men and women, and mothers with young children. A French nun whose name was on the list of those to be freed protested. She wished to remain behind and give up her place to someone else. Another French woman made the same offer, but both were refused. Idi Amin shook hands with the freed hostages, assured them that he was their friend, and wished them a good journey.

The group was taken by bus to the French consulate where, for the first time, they met their country's ambassador to Uganda. (The ambassador, Pierre Renaud, had been barred from Entebbe.) They were soon driven to the new airport facilities at Entebbe and put aboard a plane for Paris. Arriving nine hours later, they received an emotional welcome from relatives and friends.

Immediately afterward, they were interrogated by a team of French and Israeli intelligence agents. The released hostages provided valuable information, including the number of terrorists at Entebbe, the cooperative role of the Ugandan soldiers, the layout of the old terminal, and the fact that it was *not* wired with explosives. They also told of the separation of the Israelis from the other hostages, a move that was clearly interpreted as an attempt to increase the pressure on Israel.

Even before this news reached Israel, the pressure on the government had begun to mount. Anxious families of the Israeli hostages were clamoring for the government to negotiate with the terrorists. Transport Minister Yaacobi assured them at a meeting that the cabinet was well aware of the terrorists' deadline, and that its main concern was to save the lives of the hostages. The families were far from pacified. To Yaacobi it seemed that they wanted the government to abandon every consideration except the safe return of their loved ones.

Meanwhile the government was trying to exert diplomatic pressure on Idi Amin to release the hostages. The Foreign Ministry called the leaders of states sympathetic to Israel and asked them to use their influence with Amin. Israel's ambassador to the United Nations, Chaim Herzog, asked UN Secretary-General Kurt Waldheim to intercede on a personal level. France, too, was pressuring African governments and heads of state. By nightfall it was apparent that these pressures were having no effect on Amin and that the Ugandan dictator was working hand-in-glove with the terrorists. Col. Bar-Lev's telephone conversation with Amin that night dispelled any lingering notion that "Big Daddy" might be acting as a mediator between the terrorists and the Israelis. A part of that conversation follows:

Bar-Lev: "Your Excellency, until I find a way of coming to visit you, can you take every possible step to make sure that nothing happens to the hostages?"

Amin: "I'm with the leader of the PFLP now. He's only just arrived. The man I negotiated with previously was their number two. Now the right man has arrived. [This may have been Wadia Hadad.] Forty minutes ago he told me that he won't change his decision . . . . They've put high explosives around everything, outside and inside. They said that the deadline is tomorrow noon. They've already prepared everything to press the button and blow up all the hostages. They want to negotiate through France. I told them that I have some friends in Israel, like you, Gen. [Moshe] Dayan, even the prime minister, that I can negotiate with them, but they said only the French government . . . ."

To the Israelis, it now appeared obvious that Amin was the willing tool of the PFLP and that he was merely relaying its messages in the presence of its leader.

On Wednesday, too, Israel's military leaders were under mounting pressure from Defense Minister Peres to produce a feasible plan for a rescue mission. The spadework was proceeding at a desert base near Beersheba, the headquarters for Israel's Special Air and Commando Service. In an underground war room, 39-year-old Gen. Dan Shomron, a senior paratroop officer, was screening one plan after another for freeing the hostages at Entebbe. Shomron's credentials for directing airborne commando missions were impressive. As a young paratrooper, he had participated in a number of raids against guerrilla bases beyond Israel's borders. In the Six Day War (1967), he commanded a force of jeeps carrying recoilless guns that was the first Israeli unit to reach the Suez Canal. In the Yom Kippur War (1973), Shomron commanded a brigade that completed the encirclement of 25,000 troops of the Egyptian Third Corps before the UN Security Council ordered a cease-fire.

Shomron was strongly opposed to a negotiated deal with the terrorists at Entebbe, and believed that a military operation could succeed. So far, however, neither he nor any of his subordinates had been able to come up with a plan that was satisfactory to Gen. Gur. As Gen. Gur recalled, "On Wednesday morning a number of plans were submitted to me, all of them in keeping with the objectives of the operation, and all capable of hitting the terrorists. But there were weak points in all of them, so I could not clearly and single-mindedly support and recommend them as operations for execution. The main point was that I could not guarantee the safety of the hostages."

The problem, as Gen. Gur saw it, was still the same — the lack of accurate intelligence data about the layout of the airfield at Entebbe and the forces guarding it.

In the absence of a sound military plan, some Israeli leaders began to grasp at straws. Among the more bizarre proposals was one to kidnap Idi Amin. Another was to send Gen. Moshe Dayan, Israel's outstanding hero in the Six Day War, to negotiate personally with Idi Amin in Uganda. For a time, this proposal was considered seriously, and Dayan himself appeared willing to go. Prime Minister Rabin finally vetoed the idea. "I was convinced," Rabin said, "that Idi Amin was deeply involved with the terrorists, so why send Dayan to him to become another hostage? That would have given Amin his strongest bargaining point with Israel."

During the day, the pressure on the Israeli hostages at Entebbe also increased. One of them, 26-year-old Nachum Dahan, was suspected by the terrorists of being an Israeli soldier. (According to Michal Warshavsky, the terrorists feared that one or more of the hostages might be soldiers with concealed weapons in their luggage.) Dahan had aroused their suspicion because he was traveling with a French passport although his ID card was Israeli. Taken to another room, he was questioned and beaten repeatedly by Ugandan officers. They demanded that he write a report divulging everything he knew about Israel's Defense Forces. Dahan wrote a report describing life on a *kibbutz* (an Israeli cooperative farm). A Ugandan tore the report out of Dahan's hands and threw it on the floor. "This is not what we want," he said. "We want to know about the army. We want to know where its bases are. We want the name of your general." One of the Arab terrorists then put a gun to Dahan's chest by way of emphasis.

Rumors that Dahan was being beaten soon reached the other Israeli hostages. One of them, Yitzhak David, who had survived a Nazi concentration camp, protested to Wilfried Böse. "Do you see this number on my arm?" David asked the terrorist. "I got it in a German concentration camp. My parents were killed there. We thought that a new generation had grown up in Germany. But today it is difficult for us to believe that the Nazi movement died."

Böse seemed shaken by these words. Finally he replied that he belonged to the Baader-Meinhoff group in Germany which had nothing to do with Nazism. Its aim, he said, was to rid the world of capitalism. A day would come, he added, when the whole world would be one big commune.

While Dahan was being beaten, other Israelis were subjected to a more subtle form of torture. Moshe Peretz described it in his diary:

"The terrorists have invented a new form of entertainment. They read out the names of Israelis and each one who is called must raise his hand. One of the terrorists then makes some mysterious mark next to his name. Does the mark signify life or death? It's horrifying. One boy, about 16 years old, is apparently slow in raising his hand. He is rewarded by one of the Arabs with a sharp slap and terrifying shouts."

That night, the terrorists returned Nachum Dahan to the room with the other Israelis, but kept him isolated. They told him to write another report for them. Aware that Dahan was in trouble, the Israelis decided to stay awake and watch him conspicuously. Finally the German woman terrorist told Dahan to go to sleep. Only then did the other hostages also close their eyes.

As for the mattresses that Idi Amin had provided for the hostages, Mrs. Davidson made the following notation in her diary: "After taking a look at them, I have a feeling that they are full of fleas and bedbugs, so I tell Uzi that we had better go on sleeping on the floor."

VIII

ISRAEL DECIDES TO NEGOTIATE

Thursday, July 1, 1976

As the Thursday deadline for surrendering to the terrorists' demands approached, a sense of helplessness and depression pervaded Israel. The fact that the terrorists had separated the Israeli hostages from the others seemed as ominous to the public as it had to the hostages themselves. In Tel Aviv, relatives of the hostages broke into Prime Minister Rabin's office compound and demanded that the government yield to the PFLP. They reminded him that Israel's refusal to negotiate with Palestinian terrorists at the 1972 Olympic games had led to the death of all the hostages and had not stopped further terrorist acts. What the distraught relatives did not know was that Rabin and his cabinet had already reached the decision to enter into negotiations with the PFLP.

At 7:45 A.M., the government crisis team had met to review Israel's position. The ministers concluded that all diplomatic efforts to pressure Idi Amin had failed and that they had no alternative but to open negotiations with the PFLP. At 8:30, the full cabinet met and, after hearing the crisis team's decision, voted unamiously to support it. The cabinet also empowered the crisis team to direct the negotiations with the terrorists.

The government, however, was not about to capitulate completely to the PFLP. It was agreed that Israel would not discuss the release of terrorists held by other countries. Israel was prepared to release, in Prime Minister Rabin's words, "a certain number of prisoners" held in its jails in exchange for "all the hostages" held at Entebbe. In other words, the number of prisoners that the government would release was negotiable. Israel had no intention of freeing all 40 named by the PFLP.

Following the meeting, a number of ministers privately expressed the belief that the decision to negotiate some of the PFLP's demands would benefit Israel in two ways. First, it would safeguard the lives of the hostages at Entebbe. Second, it would give Israel more time to prepare a military operation should one prove necessary. Rabin himself did not rule out the possibility of a military mission even after the decision was made to negotiate. "We continued to prepare our military option," he said later, "in case the negotiations would end [break down] or be dragged out by the other side."

The government had acted early in the day so that the terrorists could be informed of its decision before their noon deadline. Meanwhile, Col. Bar-Lev had again called Idi Amin to discuss a personal meeting with him in Uganda. This time Amin's answer was rather startling. "Inform your government officially," he said sternly, "that the PFLP will make an announcement at 11 A.M. That's the only answer I can give you. These are instructions that I received from the Front [PFLP]. OK? We had very difficult talks until now. It's best that you wait for the announcement."

Defense Minister Peres was encouraged by this message from Amin. If the terrorists were planning to do anything drastic at Entebbe, Amin would have strongly urged Bar-Lev to have his government take some ameliorative action before the announcement. Instead, he told Bar-Lev, "It isn't necessary that you come to Uganda. If you have something extremely important to tell me, listen to the announcement, phone me, and I'll tell you what to do."

The announcement, which was broadcast by Radio Uganda, stated that the PFLP had decided to extend its deadline until 11 A.M. on Sunday. It made no mention at all of the Israeli government's decision that morning to negotiate. Undoubtedly, the PFLP announcement was made *before* news of Israel's decision reached it.

By extending its deadline to Sunday, the PFLP relieved the immediate pressure on Israel. But by another action that it took later, the PFLP made certain that Israel's relief would be very brief. At 2 P.M., the terrorists released 101 of the hostages at Entebbe. All of them were non-Israelis. Of the remaining hostages, 83 were Israelis and another 20 were dual citizens of Israel and France. Transport Minister Yaacobi summed up the situation tersely when he said, *"Israel is the target."*

The remaining hostages were not friendless. Captain Bacos, the French pilot of Flight 139, insisted that he and his crew (12 altogether) would not leave Entebbe until *all* of the hostages had safely departed, and he kept to his word. Throughout the ordeal at Entebbe, Captain Bacos' behavior was exemplary. According to the hostages, Bacos attended the sick, dispensed medicine, made beds, and even swept the floor. While keeping up the hostages' morale, he cautioned them not to engage in political arguments with the terrorists that might provoke reprisals. Bacos also wrote a detailed report on the hijacking of Flight 139 that he forwarded to Paris with some of the released hostages. "It was a dangerous action," an Israeli minister commented, "dangerous to his own safety. But it was characteristic of all his actions."

That afternoon, the Israeli government's crisis

team met to discuss the new developments. The ministers concluded that, with the release of all non-Israeli hostages, the terrorists' confrontation was now with Israel alone. Whether the solution to the problem would be political or military, Israel would have to bear the full responsibility.

The man who was pushing hardest for a military solution, Defense Minister Peres, met afterward with Gen. Shomron and other top officers of Israel's paratroop and commando forces. Peres expressed his conviction that even without complete intelligence about Entebbe, the risks of a military operation were worth taking. In all of Israel's anti-terrorist operations, he said, there had always been some "blind spots." The main difference now was not so much the lack of information about Entebbe, but the very long distance involved. "Once you can negotiate the distance," he said, "you must take the same risks as you would back home." All but one of the officers, who said he wanted to think about it more, concurred with Peres' judgment. Shomron said he was certain that a military operation would be "one hundred per cent successful. We have done things a thousand times more complicated."

Then Peres asked the officers what day would be the earliest that a military operation could be carried out. All agreed that it would be possible by Saturday. Peres told them to work on a plan calling for a midnight Saturday landing at Entebbe.

"By the evening," Gen. Gur recalled, "we indeed had a certain plan, but I must say that I could not yet offer it [to the cabinet] as operative, and there were still aspects of it that I called 'charlatan and irresponsible.' I explained that I was not about to recommend the plan until there was additional [intelligence] data."

Nevertheless, Gen. Gur did give his approval for a "dress rehearsal" of the plan; it would be staged the next night at an Israeli air base. In effect, Gen. Gur was saying, "Show me."

At 11 P.M., the crisis team met again to discuss the tactics of negotiation with the terrorists. A suggestion was made that the technical aspects of a prisoner exchange should be discussed first. Where would the exchange take place? Whose planes would be used to transport prisoners? How would the actual exchange be managed? The crisis team agreed that negotiations should open on these questions. Until they could be answered satisfactorily, there would be no discussion of the number of terrorists to be released or their names. As a first step, Israel's negotiators suggested to the French Foreign Ministry that the exchange take place on French territory. (The PFLP had demanded that it take place at Entebbe.)

At Entebbe, the day had also begun in a mood of helplessness and despair. Nachum Dahan was again questioned, this time by Arab terrorists who had found in his luggage pictures of him sitting on a battle tank. Dahan's explanation

— that the pictures were taken by a friend when they chanced upon an Israeli tank — failed to satisfy the terrorists. Once again he was beaten and knocked to the floor. The terrorists demanded that he tell them about his role in the army. "Do you want to live or die?" one of them asked him. Dahan was ordered to write another report. He filled 11 pages with a description of life in Paris.

At noon, Idi Amin appeared with his young son, Gamal Abdel Nasser, who was named after the late president of Egypt. Father and son were dressed in identical uniforms, camouflaged battle fatigues that were pressed very neatly. Amin told the Israelis that he was negotiating with his good friend Col. Bar-Lev, and that he had gained an extension of the terrorists' deadline to 11 A.M. Sunday. The news failed to impress the Israelis. They made no response and appeared quite depressed.

When the non-Israeli hostages left two hours later, the Israelis were moved back to the main passenger lounge. There they were reunited with the French crew and 20 other hostages of dual French and Israeli citizenship. At 6 P.M., Captain Bacos told the remaining hostages that the government of Israel had accepted the PFLP's demands "in their entirety." (Whatever the source of his information, it was far from correct.) This is how Moshe Peretz described the hostages' reaction in his diary:

"What joy! Everyone is hugging and kissing one another, as though they had just been born anew."

The hostages were sure now that they would be released within a few hours. Nevertheless, some among them had misgivings about Israel's apparent "surrender" to the terrorists. "We wanted to go home, of course," Michal Warshavsky remembered. "But we knew that surrender was bad for Israel. We thought, in another week the terrorists will hijack another airplane, and then another — it will never end. At the moment, however, what would happen next week did not seem important."

Mrs. Davidson went to sleep that night confident that her family's ordeal would soon be over. Before retiring, she made this entry in her diary: "More mattresses are brought us. I don't care any more about the bedbugs and fleas. We've had enough of sleeping on the floor. If we aren't released tonight, we'll sleep on the mattresses."

IX

A MILITARY ALTERNATIVE TAKES SHAPE

Friday, July 2, 1976

Was Israel's decision to negotiate with the PFLP genuine or was it a ruse to stall for time? Prime Minister Rabin later told the Knesset (parliament) that "We were prepared to adopt even this alternative [negotiations] — in default of any other — to rescue our people. This was not a tactic to gain time, and had this choice alone been left, we would have stood by our decision as a last resort."

As Friday morning began, nothing had yet happened to persuade Rabin that a military operation was feasible. The tentative plan for a military mission that Gen. Gur had already rejected as in some aspects "charlatan and irresponsible" was also turned down by Rabin. On this occasion Rabin had said, "I want no rescue operation with soldiers holding one-way tickets. I want proof that the first plane into Entebbe can land safely and get back. A catastrophe will be the most tremendous victory for our enemies."

Rabin was not speaking as a military novice. In Israel's War of Independence, he had served as a brigade commander and afterward studied at British Staff College, a military school for training advanced officers. In 1963, Rabin was appointed Chief of Staff of Israel's Defense Forces and held that post during the Six Day War. So Rabin's judgment was based as much upon sound military considerations as it was upon a humane regard for the lives of Israel's hostages and soldiers. Perhaps the proof that Rabin required before consenting to a military operation would come that night when Israel's Special Air and Commando Service was scheduled to test its rescue plan.

Both before and after the Friday night dress rehearsal, vital information about Entebbe began reaching Israel's intelligence chiefs. From Washington, D.C., the Pentagon had sent photographs of the Entebbe area taken by space satellites. Israeli agents forwarded pictures of Entebbe taken by spy planes. On-the-ground photos of the airport's facilities were sent by black intelligence agents who had infiltrated from Kenya. In Israel, the Solel Boneh construction company pulled out blueprints it had used to build new sections of the airport during the period of cooperation between Israel and Uganda. Using all of this material, engineers of the construction company built a rough, full-scale model of Entebbe Airport to train commandos for a raid.

On Friday, too, another problem crucial to a

military operation was solved: Where would Israel's rescue planes be allowed to land and refuel on their return trip from Entebbe? Most of the route Israeli planes would have to fly was lined by hostile Arab and African countries. But Kenya, which borders Uganda on the east, was in relatively friendly hands. President Jomo Kenyatta of Kenya had been very wary of Idi Amin since the previous March. At that time, Amin had claimed that a large area of Kenya rightfully belonged to Uganda. Kenyatta had responded with a speech saying that his country was ready to go to war to protect its boundaries. Kenyatta was also incensed by the PFLP's demand that he release five terrorists who had conspired to shoot down an Israeli airliner at Nairobi Airport in January, 1976. Undoubtedly Amin himself had given the PFLP their names.

Israel thought that Kenyatta might be receptive to a commando strike against Entebbe, especially if it should also succeed in destroying Russian MIG fighter planes stationed there. That would help reduce the odds against Kenya if Idi Amin should attempt to annex Kenyan territory. So Israel approached the government of Kenya for permission to refuel its planes at Nairobi Airport in the event of a military operation.

Kenyan officials were aware that if they cooperated with Israel in a military venture against Uganda, it would certainly arouse the anger of other African nations. But what if the laws governing international civil aviation were stretched a little? Long-range military aircraft are required to carry civilian markings that serve, in effect, as international license plates. (Israel's international code marking is 4X plus the number of the plane.) So if Israeli planes were to identify themselves with civilian markings and ask the control tower at Nairobi Airport for permission to land, how could they be refused? In this manner the problem was resolved, and Kenya gave its assurance that an Israeli airborne force would be allowed to land and refuel at Nairobi. To make sure that there would be no interference with the refueling operation, Kenyan security forces would be stationed all around the El Al Israel facilities at the airport. (After the raid, Kenya vehemently denied cooperating with the Israelis, and Gen. Gur told diplomats and news correspondents that "We forced ourselves on the Kenyans.")

Meanwhile Israel was learning more about security conditions at Entebbe. According to its intelligence reports, the terminal was guarded by no more than 80-100 Ugandan soldiers, plus 10 terrorists. Moreover, the Ugandans seemed quite lax in their guard duties. Obviously they were not expecting any unwelcome visitors, especially from a distance of 2,500 miles. More and more, Entebbe appeared vulnerable to a swift, audacious commando attack. As one Israeli official commented, "Militarily, the situation at Entebbe now looks easier than those times when Palestinians held hostages here in Israel."

As the day progressed, Israel was beginning to lean toward a military operation. Everything would hinge upon the outcome of the dress rehearsal that its paratroop and commando forces would stage that night for Gen. Gur.

For the hostages at Entebbe, that Friday had begun with a severe jolt to their hopes for an early release. At 7 A.M., Idi Amin entered the terminal accompanied by one of his wives and his son, Gamal. Amin told the hostages that Israel had *not* accepted the PFLP's demands, and that their situation was very grave. The terrorists, he said, had surrounded the building with TNT, and would blow it up unless Israel capitulated. Then he announced that he was leaving to attend a meeting in Mauritius of the Organization of African States, but would be back before Sunday (when the terrorists' deadline was due to expire). He advised the hostages to write a letter in the meantime asking their government to accept the PFLP's conditions. He urged that the letter be ready for broadcast by Radio Uganda at 1 P.M.

When Amin left, a heated argument developed among the hostages as to whether or not they should write the letter he had asked for. Many men who had families, as well as the French crew (except Captain Bacos), favored writing the letter. Others, led by Yitzhak David, the former concentration camp prisoner, opposed it. The argument continued for hours, taxing the nerves of the distraught hostages. Moshe Peretz wrote in his diary, "The ebb and flow of feelings is breaking people, bringing them to the threshold of collapse."

Eventually the hostages decided upon a compromise. They would write a letter, but word it in such a way that it would not put undue pressure on their government. The letter, which was written by a committee, thanked Idi Amin for his "fair treatment" of the hostages and urged the government of Israel to work for their release. It was handed to the terrorists in the evening.

While the letter-writing was going on, a 19-year-old Israeli named Jean-Jacques Maimoni did his best to dispel the gloom in the terminal. Exuding good cheer, Maimoni set up a "bar" and offered to make any kind of drink the hostages asked for. There were calls for whiskey and soda, fresh orange juice, and milk shakes, among others. Of course, Maimoni could give his "customers" the only beverages available, coffee or tea, but everyone enjoyed the game.

Mrs. Davidson found some relief performing housekeeping chores. "We are allowed to do some washing," she wrote in her diary, "and the Ugandans have strung up some clothes lines in the small court where we take our daily walk. A pity we aren't allowed to wash ourselves; I think we really need a bath."

A mishap occurred during the day that later would have tragic consequences. While eating lunch, Dora Bloch almost choked when a bone lodged in her throat. A Ugandan doctor recommended that the 75-year-old woman be taken to a hospital in Kampala for treatment. She was still in the hospital when the commando raid at Entebbe took place. The next day, according to witnesses, she was dragged from her bed by three men dressed as hospital employes. She has never been seen or heard from since, and is presumed dead.

Sundown on Friday marked the beginning of the Jewish Sabbath. Moshe Peretz made the following note in his diary: "We sang Sabbath songs, quietly, because those outside [the terrorists] were touchy, especially in the evening."

As the Sabbath began in Israel, it had special significance for the paratroop and commando units that were assembled at a desert air base to prove to Gen. Gur that they could carry out a successful rescue mission in Uganda. For Gen. Gur, two problems were central. First, did the pilots and navigators have the know-how to arrive at a precise destination 2,500 miles away without the benefit of navigational aid from the ground? There could be no radio communication at all between Israeli bases and the rescue planes once the aircraft took off. Any radio traffic would certainly be monitored by hostile intelligence forces, and the success of the mission depended upon complete surprise. The second problem that concerned Gen. Gur was how quickly the commandos could reach the hostages once the planes landed at Entebbe. Unless the commandos got inside the terminal within an estimated 75 seconds or less, the hostages would surely be slaughtered. And a not insignificant force of about 100 soldiers and guerrillas was guarding the terminal.

That evening, Gen. Gur climbed aboard a giant Lockheed C-130 Hercules transport plane with Gen. Benny Peled, chief of the Israeli Air Force, for a two-hour test flight. The C-130 was almost uniquely suited for the mission that Israel was now considering. With a radar unit in its nose and instrument panels equipped with the most sophisticated navigational aids, it can fly in any weather and without visibility. It is powered by four propjet engines that, at the height of their power, actually sound muffled. (This would be an important asset in the Entebbe raid.) Though the plane has a takeoff weight of 155,000 pounds, it can lift off the ground in eight seconds after a run of only 800 feet. It can also land — and has — on a runway no longer than that of an aircraft carrier. With a wingspan of 132 feet, it is capable of airlifting more than 45,000 pounds of cargo, or 64 paratroopers with their full complement of weapons and vehicles.

In the course of the test flight, Gen. Gur posed a number of complex problems for the pilot and navigator to see whether they could solve them without any external help. Later Gen. Gur recalled, "They spoke quietly and confidently and impressed me with their navigational capabilities and powers of improvisation. This gave me the feeling that, as far as the air aspect was concerned, it would be all right. If there were any hitches in the plan, these boys would be able to overcome them."

Later Gen. Gur talked to the commando units that had been conducting ground exercises all day. They told him that they were confident they could carry out the rescue mission within one hour. "Better make that 55 minutes," Gen. Gur replied. Once again the commandos rehearsed their assignments, racing down the ramp of a Hercules, and fanning out in simulated attacks on Ugandan troops, the control tower, and most important, the old terminal building. By this time, the team of sharpshooters assigned to free the hostages knew the layout of the terminal as well as they knew their own homes.

Afterward Gen. Gur spoke with Dan Shomron and other officers who had been rehearsing the plan. All of them expressed confidence in their ability to carry out the operation with maximum results.

"The feeling I got from all the men who would be on the spot at Entebbe," Gen. Gur recalled, "who would have to deal with the terrorists and hit them before they hit the hostages, was unmistakeably positive. And so I felt that, with some minor corrections, I could recommend this plan as operational the following morning."

Then it would be up to Israel's defense leaders to persuade Prime Minister Rabin that a commando raid 2,500 miles from home was indeed feasible.

X

OPERATION THUNDERBALL

Saturday and Sunday, July 3 and 4, 1976

Israel's attack force began assembling early Saturday morning, although there was no certainty yet that Prime Minister Rabin and the cabinet would approve the mission. Most of the officers were convinced that the government was committed to a policy of negotiations, which to them meant surrender. Even as they grumbled about "the politicians," the officers rushed the preparations for their mission — just in case.

The mission already had a name, "Thunderball," which came from a computer. The mission also had a commander. To no one's surprise, it was Dan Shomron, the man who had sweated most over the planning for Thunderball. Second in command was 30-year-old Jonathan (Yonni) Netanyahu, who headed an elite paratroop unit that was assigned to free the hostages in the terminal. Yonni had been born in the United States, but was raised in Israel. Wounded in the Six Day War, he was discharged from the army with a 30% disability. Yonni came to the United States for medical treatment and afterward took a postgraduate course in philosophy at Harvard. On his return to Israel, he rejoined the army as a commando. Two months before Thunderball, he was assigned to lead a special antiterrorist combat unit composed of crack marksmen. Because Yonni was a keen student of the Scriptures and ancient Israel, he was given a Hebrew nickname that meant "the man of the sword and the Bible."

The work of loading the mission's four C-130 Hercules transport planes was going ahead. Jeeps with recoilless guns, light armored personnel carriers, and trucks were driven up the broad ramps at the rear of each Hercules and cradled inside. Bazooka rockets, grenades, radio equipment and other supplies were also stowed aboard the four "flying boxcars."

Soon another vehicle was ready to mount a Hercules ramp. This was not the kind of vehicle that would ordinarily take part in a military operation. But the Israelis are not ordinary people, and this was not an ordinary mission. The vehicle was a shiny, black Mercedes, identical in every detail to the limousine used by Idi Amin in Kampala. Only the night before, it had been a white Mercedes, but the commandos who "drafted" the car from its owner had expertly sprayed it black.

Another cosmetic job was being done that morning by a make-up artist on a burly Israeli paratrooper. When the job was completed, the paratrooper bore an astonishing resemblance to "Big Daddy" Amin. Other commandos were dressed to look like Amin's Palestinian bodyguards. All these preparations had but one aim: to get a number of commandos, disguised as Idi Amin and his bodyguards, past the Ugandan troops at Entebbe Airport without having to fire a shot. (After the raid, Gen. Gur declined to comment on the ruse, but did admit that the commandos used "several tricks.")

That morning Defense Minister Peres visited the base, checked the latest intelligence reports, and assured the commandos that their rehearsal the night before would not prove to be a waste of either time or money. As Defense Minister, Peres had the authority to move military forces anywhere within Israel's frontiers. Now he told Gen. Shomron and his men to fly to Sharm el Sheikh, the site of Israel's southernmost air base, as soon as their preparations were completed.

At 11:30, the government crisis team met in Tel Aviv, and Peres forcefully urged approval of a commando raid on Entebbe. The man who would have to bear full responsibility for the outcome — and lose his job if the raid proved a disaster for Israel — was, of course, Prime Minister Rabin. After asking some hard questions about the plan, Rabin gave his consent. Only one more step remained — the approval of the full cabinet.

The cabinet was scheduled to meet at 2 P.M. Two of the ministers were Orthodox Jews whose religious scruples forbade them to use any kind of transportation on the Sabbath. Though one of them had a 90-minute walk from his home in the suburbs, he declined the use of a chauffeur-driven car offered by Rabin and made it to the meeting on foot.

So far, the military planning and preparations had been conducted with such secrecy that most of the cabinet ministers did not even know of them. It was necessary for Gen. Gur to describe the operation in detail and then answer questions about it. Some members of the cabinet were concerned about the possible loss of lives, but Rabin fought strongly in favor of the raid "even if 10, 20, or 25 are killed."

The timetable for the mission called for the planes to leave Sharm el Sheikh at 3:30 P.M. At three o'clock, the cabinet was still deliberating. Fearful of any further delay, Rabin authorized Peres to send the planes off. One condition was imposed: If the cabinet voted against the raid, the planes would have to turn back. For the commandos, the suspense was almost unbearable. "The ministers talk while we sweat," one of them remarked. "Why in hell can't they just tell us to go?" At 3:30, the cabinet voted unanimously in favor of the raid. By that time, the planes were already on their way.

While these events were taking place in Israel, the despair of the hostages at Entebbe was deepening. Many of them were sure now that they would soon be slaughtered. The terrorists were becoming increasingly nervous and sullen as the Sunday deadline approached. The complicated chain of communications with Israel's negotiators had been complicated even more by Idi Amin's absence from Uganda. By Saturday, the negotiations seemed to be stalled. The PFLP was still insisting on the release of all 53 prisoners it had named originally. Israel's negotiating team in Paris, completely unaware of the military preparations at home, was still holding out for considerably fewer. West Germany also appeared very reluctant to release any of the prisoners in its custody, though it would have done so if pressed by Israel.

Ilan Hartuv recalled the mood of the terrorists at this time: "I felt sure that even if the terrorists would have agreed to two or three days more of negotiations, it still would have ended in disaster for us. Both the German woman and this fellow Jaber [Fayez Abdul-Rahim Jaber, one of the terrorists], whom we nicknamed 'The Cruel One,' had their fingers itching on the trigger . . . I was sure they wanted very much to find some pretext to kill us."

Hartuv's fears were not unjustified. On his way to the toilet that morning, Hartuv was stopped by Jaber and accused of plotting against the PFLP. (This suspicion had been aroused by Hartuv's frequent conversations with Idi Amin.) The terrorist forced Hartuv to stand in a puddle of water outside the terminal. When Hartuv protested, Jaber clicked a bullet into the chamber of his weapon. "I froze," Hartuv recalled later. "It was a terrifying moment." Fortunately, another terrorist, probably Bouvier, interceded and Hartuv's life was spared.

To add to their mental anguish, most of the hostages were suffering from diarrhea and nausea, the result of eating spoiled food. The toilets were clogged, and sanitary conditions were dreadful. Some hostages, who were retching uncontrollably, had to be taken to a nearby dispensary for treatment. Others lay immobile on their foul mattresses.

Late that afternoon, Idi Amin returned from Mauritius and paid the hostages another visit. He was wearing an air force uniform with his Israeli paratrooper's wings and a blue beret. Amin told the hostages that the Israeli government was to blame for their fate because it had not fulfilled the terrorists' demands. "Your government is gambling with your lives," he warned them as he left. It was the last time the hostages would see the Ugandan dictator.

At this time, the Israeli rescue force was already more than one hour from its base at Sharm el Sheikh, flying south over the Red Sea. This was the regular route flown by commercial airliners to central and south Africa. If hostile radar surveillance screens detected the flight, it would not appear as anything unusual. Moving ahead of the slower Lockheed C-130 transport planes were two Boeing 707 jets, each with a different mission. One would function as a command plane and communications center at Entebbe. Circling over the airport, it would pick up all radio messages transmitted by the commando units on the ground. If any problems arose, Gen. Peled and Gen. Yekutiel Adam (Israel's Deputy Chief of Staff) would be able to provide fast solutions. The other Boeing 707 carried a team of 23 doctors and nurses with the most modern medical equipment available. This plane would serve as a hospital unit at Nairobi Airport to care for those who might be wounded at Entebbe.

Both 707's landed at El Al Israel's Nairobi facility without attracting attention. Gen. Peled's plane quickly refueled and took off again for Entebbe. The hospital plane, of course, remained at Nairobi to prepare for its mission. A smaller medical unit was aboard one of the C-130's to give emergency treatment at Entebbe.

All the planes encountered thunderstorms along the way, but had to fly through them to conserve fuel. At the base of the Red Sea, they banked west on a course that would take them across Ethiopia, Kenya, and finally Lake Victoria, the approach to Entebbe. During the seven-hour trip, Dan Shomron and Yonni Netanyahu went over the details of the operation again and again. The plan called for their C-130 transport to land first. It would touch down on a newly-built runway and come to a halt about a half-mile from the old terminal. Shomron was convinced that if the lead plane could land safely without alerting the terrorists, the operation would succeed.

How could a huge transport plane — followed by three others — hope to land at Entebbe Airport without being detected by the control tower's radar unit? Because details of the raid are still kept secret by Israel, there has been considerable speculation about this. One theory is that the lead plane announced itself to the control tower as an Air France flight bringing in terrorists released from Israel's jails. This seems highly improbable. Such an announcement, in fact, would have alerted the entire airport and brought Idi Amin rushing to the scene. (At the moment, Amin was asleep at his residence in Kampala.) A much more plausible explanation offered by knowledgeable informants is this: As the four transports approached Entebbe from Lake Victoria, they descended almost to the water level, and came in at zero altitude—below the range of conventional radar. Once the planes reached the airport's runways, engines were cut so that the men in the control tower probably didn't even hear the C-130's touch down. Idi Amin was highly incensed by their failure to detect the Israeli force; all four controllers were summarily shot hours later.

The lead plane braked quietly to a halt a few minutes after midnight, Ugandan time. It was within 30 seconds of the target time set by the operational plan. A half-mile away was the old

terminal building, which the terrorists kept
lighted at night. Everything depended now on
the speed with which the commandos could get to
it. The big door at the rear of the plane opened
and dropped down to the ground, becoming a
ramp. The first vehicle to drive out was the black
Mercedes carrying a passenger who could hardly
be distinguished from Idi Amin. Close behind it
were two Land-Rovers manned by paratroopers
dressed as Amin's Palestinian bodyguards. As
the small motorcade rolled toward the floodlit
area surrounding the terminal, Ugandan guards
snapped to attention, convinced that their president was paying another visit to the hostages.
Meanwhile three other commando units poured
out of the Hercules transports in jeeps and other
vehicles. The first unit, led by Shomron and
Yonni Netanyahu, raced toward the hostages.
Along the way it encountered a patrol of Ugandan
soldiers who, in Shomron's words, were "quickly
eliminated." The other units rapidly spread out
to gain control of the entire airport.

The sudden arrival of Israeli commandos at the
old terminal building took the terrorists completely by surprise. It is doubtful whether any of
them ever imagined that Israel would send a
military mission so far. Most of them didn't even
have time to react. The first terrorist was killed
by gunfire outside the entrance. Simultaneously,
the commandos burst into the building. Two terrorists immediately to the left of the entrance
were shot down as they tried to snap in their

ammunition clips. (One of them was the German woman, Gabriele Kroche-Tiedemann.) Wilfried Böse, on the far left, aimed his submachine gun but apparently froze with fear. He was gunned down before he could squeeze the trigger of his own weapon. A fourth terrorist on the far right managed to fire a few shots at the Israelis, but failed to hit any of them. Wounded by a commando, he crumpled to the floor, attempted to rise, but then was hit again. According to Gen. Gur, the four terrorists inside the entrance were killed within 45 seconds. Other commandos raced up to the second floor and killed two more terrorists who were hiding in a toilet. Three terrorists, including Antonio Bouvier, were not found. The Israelis believe they slipped out a back door and escaped.

The quick elimination of the terrorists did not mean the shooting was over. Ugandan soldiers were firing at the Israelis from the second floor and roof of the terminal, as well as from the control tower. The Israelis were returning their fire with bazooka rockets, submachine guns, grenades, and rifles. Yonni Netanyahu was directing the Israeli fire outside the terminal, standing with his back to the control tower. A Ugandan soldier on the tower took aim and fired. Yonni fell to the ground face down, bleeding profusely. "Yonni's been hit!" one of the commandos shouted, and called for a "medic." It was too late to help Yonni. "The man of the sword and the Bible" was dead, the only Israeli soldier to lose his life in the raid. (The mission was later renamed "Operation Jonathan" in his honor.)

Meanwhile another team of commandos had taken off for a corner of the airfield where approximately 10 Russian MIG fighter planes were located. The MIGs were systematically blown up, either with explosive charges or bazooka rockets. After the raid, Gen. Gur stated that the MIGs were destroyed only when Ugandan soldiers in the vicinity opened fire on Israeli commandos trying to gain control of the airport. It is much more likely, however, that the MIGs had been earmarked for destruction in the Israeli operational plan. The Israelis certainly had a number of good reasons to destroy them. One was to prevent pursuit and interception of the rescue force after it left Entebbe. Another was to prevent their use for training Palestinian pilots sworn to the destruction of Israel. A third reason was to prevent their use against Kenya, which had cooperated with Israel by permitting its planes to land and refuel at Nairobi Airport.

When the first shots were fired outside the terminal, most of the hostages were getting ready to sleep, or were already asleep. Their first reactions were mixed, but no one remotely believed Israeli soldiers had come to rescue them. Some hostages thought that Idi Amin had ordered his soldiers to free them; Ugandan troops were probably firing at the terrorists. Others believed the worst had come; the terrorists were starting to execute hostages outside. One woman hostage remembered thinking, "If I am going to die, please let it be quick."

When the shooting intensified, panic broke out. Many hostages ran or crept to the toilets, seeking an illusory "safety." Others threw themselves down on their mattresses. Mothers and fathers flung themselves on top of their children to shield them from bullets. As the commandos burst into the terminal, they shouted, "We are Israelis! Lie down!" Even then some hostages failed to understand what was happening, or were unable to hear the commandos amid all the shooting. In any event, a number of them ignored the warnings to lie down and were hit by gunfire. Were they, as Gen. Gur explained later, caught in the crossfire between commandos and terrorists? Or were they fired upon by the commandos who, in the excitement of the moment, mistook them for terrorists? In all likelihood, casualties occurred both ways.

Three hostages were killed and a number of others wounded. The dead were Pasco Cohen, who had survived a Nazi concentration camp and all of Israel's wars; Jean-Jacques Maimoni, who had tried to lift the hostages' morale by setting up a "bar"; and Ida Borowicz, 56, who was hit by a stray bullet and also suffered a heart attack during the assault.

When all resistance was crushed outside the terminal, an Israeli paratrooper made an announcement by loudspeaker. "It's OK now," he said. "You are going home. There is a plane waiting for you."

Outside, the night was cool and clear. Within minutes, all the hostages and the French crew had reached the C-130 Hercules that would fly them to Israel. Some were driven to it in open command cars, others walked or ran the distance of 300 yards. Once they were inside and counted, the rear door slammed shut and the plane began to move. From the time the first Hercules landed at Entebbe until this moment, 53 minutes had elapsed. The Israelis accomplished their mission in two minutes less than their timetable had called for.

There were no celebrations aboard the plane. Most of the hostages were still too dazed and shocked as a result of the shootout to engage in any kind of revelry. Some of them had left the terminal in such haste they were still wearing pajamas or were only half-dressed. They sat in stunned silence, their spirits depressed by the stretchers at the rear on which the wounded and the dead were lying. All week long Mrs. Davidson had had to be strong for the sake of her young children. Now she broke down and wept for several minutes. When she recovered, she looked around at the Israeli soldiers for the first time. About 12 of them were accompanying the hostages back to Israel. Without their battle gear, she thought, "They look like little boys." Most of them, in fact, had been conscripted at 18 to serve until they were 21. Before long, the soldiers stretched out and were fast asleep. For them, it had been a long night's work.

The C-130 Hercules touched down at Nairobi Airport to refuel and transfer the seriously wounded to the Boeing 707 hospital unit. Shortly after noon, July 4, the exhausted hostages arrived at Ben-Gurion Airport, where their nightmare journey had begun. News of the commando raid's success had elated Israel, and huge, exuberant crowds were on hand to greet them. As the hostages descended the ramp of their plane, they were literally mobbed by relatives, friends, and well-wishers. Uzi Davidson remarked to his wife, "If they didn't kill us at Entebbe, they'll do it here."

The wave of national joy touched off by the hostages' homecoming was unlike anything Israel had experienced since its victory in the Six Day War. Even the loss of four hostages and one soldier could not alter the dominant mood of jubilance and pride. One Israeli citizen summed up the feelings of his compatriots when he said, "We answered the terrorists' blackmail with good old Jewish *chutzpah*." (Chutzpah is a Jewish word meaning "nerve.") Dan Shomron, who led the commando raid at Entebbe, took a larger view.

"It was a mission," he said, "that belongs to all the people, not only in Israel, but all the people around the world who care about freedom. This was their operation. We, in a way, had the privilege of carrying it out."

XI

A SUCCESSFUL GAMBLE

The whole story of the Israeli government's deliberations after the hijacking of Flight 139, its negotiations with the PFLP, and its ultimate decision to send a military mission to Entebbe probably will not be known for several years. As long as Israel feels threatened by its Arab neighbors, it will continue to veil in secrecy as many of the circumstances of the Entebbe affair as it can. Even without access to first-hand information about the government's response to the hijacking, however, it is possible to draw some conclusions about it. These conclusions are based upon whatever information the government has made available, investigations by news reporters, and discussions that this writer had with knowledgeable Israelis.

1. From the moment the government learned of the hijacking, it began to explore the possibility of a military mission. Because of the problems

created by Uganda's great distance from Israel, the development of a military operation required time. Meanwhile the government hoped that diplomatic pressure brought to bear on Idi Amin by France and other powers might bring about a release of the hostages. It soon became apparent that Amin was cooperating fully with the terrorists and that diplomatic pressure was useless.

2. The terrorists made known their demands on Tuesday, June 29, two days after they had hijacked Flight 139. The fact that 40 of the 53 prisoners whose release the PFLP demanded were in Israel's custody was the first indication that Israel was the primary, if not the exclusive, target of the terrorists. The government was extremely loathe to free such a large number of prisoners, and especially those who had been convicted of really heinous crimes. At that point, the pressure upon Israel's Defense Forces to produce a feasible military plan was considerably increased, especially by Defense Minister Peres.

3. Nothing stiffened the government's opposition to negotiating with the PFLP more than the news that the terrorists had separated the Israeli hostages from the non-Israeli hostages on Tuesday night. To Israel's leaders, this was reminiscent of the tragic experience of Jews in Nazi death camps, and they found it intolerable. Peres expressed their feelings quite plainly: "The mental picture of a German woman and man again threatening with guns the lives of innocent people

whose only crime is that they are Jewish is something Israel cannot stand for."

4. By Thursday morning, the Defense Forces had been unable to produce a plan that would safeguard the lives of the hostages in the event of a raid. With the terrorists' deadline only hours away, the government had no alternative but to enter into negotiations with the PFLP. But the government never abandoned its hopes for a military solution. The ministers were aware that, if the negotiations were prolonged, time would be gained to prepare a military mission. So negotiations would be opened, but only as a last resort would they be consummated.

5. The government got its first real break when the PFLP, acting before it had received word of Israel's decision, announced an extension of its deadline to Sunday. By Thursday night, the Defense Forces had developed a tentative operational plan, which was solidified on Friday by the arrival of substantial information about Entebbe Airport and the forces guarding it. When the "dress rehearsal" on Friday night proved successful, it was a foregone conclusion that the government would authorize a military operation the next day. As Prime Minister Rabin told an aide, "You fight terrorism in Zion Square in Jerusalem, or you fight it in Entebbe, but you fight. You don't give in."

Given a reasonable chance to succeed in a military gamble, the government of Israel took it — and won.

Bibliography

Books

Eban, Abba. *My Country: The Story of Modern Israel*. New York: Random House, 1972.

Lucas, Noah. *The Modern History of Israel*. New York: Praeger Publishers, 1975.

Luttwak, Edward and Horowitz, Dan. *The Israeli Army*. New York: Harper & Row, 1975.

McKnight, Gerald. *The Terrorist Mind*. Indianapolis / New York: The Bobbs-Merrill Company, 1974.

Parry, Albert. *Terrorism: From Robespierre to Arafat*. New York: The Vanguard Press, 1976.

Stevenson, William. *90 Minutes at Entebbe*. New York: Bantam Books, 1976.

Newspapers and Periodicals

Ross, Philip. "The Illustrated Story of the Great Israeli Rescue," *New York* (August 2, 1976).

Newsweek (July 19, 1976) pps. 42-46.

Time (July 19, 1976) pps. 28-30.

The Jerusalem Post (June 28-July 10, 1976).

The New York Times (June 28-July 5, 1976).

Television News

CBS-TV (September 14, 1976). "Rescue At Entebbe: How They Saved The Hostages," produced by CBS News.